HAPPINESS
HACKS

300+ Simple Ways to Get—and Stay—Happy

Adams Media

New York   London   Toronto   Sydney   New Delhi

Adams Media
An Imprint of Simon & Schuster, Inc.
57 Littlefield Street
Avon, Massachusetts 02322

First Adams Media trade paperback edition JANUARY 2018

ADAMS MEDIA and colophon are trademarks of Simon and Schuster.

For information about special discounts for bulk purchases, please contact Simon & Schuster Special Sales at 1-866-506-1949 or business@simonandschuster.com.

The Simon & Schuster Speakers Bureau can bring authors to your live event. For more information or to book an event contact the Simon & Schuster Speakers Bureau at 1-866-248-3049 or visit our website at www.simonspeakers.com.

Interior design by Katrina Machado

Manufactured in the United States of America

10 9 8 7 6 5 4 3 2 1

Library of Congress Cataloging-in-Publication Data
Adams Media (firm), issuing body.
Happiness hacks.
Avon, Massachusetts: Adams Media, 2018.
LCCN 2017043755 | ISBN 9781507206348 (pb) | ISBN 9781507206355 (ebook)
LCSH: Happiness.
LCC BF575.H27 H3669 2018 | DDC 152.4/2--dc23
LC record available at https://lccn.loc.gov/2017043755

ISBN 978-1-5072-0634-8
ISBN 978-1-5072-0635-5 (ebook)

Contains material adapted from the following title published by Adams Media, an Imprint of Simon & Schuster, Inc.: *365 Ways to Live Happy* by Meera Lester, copyright © 2010, ISBN 978-1-60550-028-7.

CONTENTS

INTRODUCTION

Are you looking to get happy? You've come to the right place.

Happiness. Everyone seems to want it and people spend their lives searching for it…yet it often seems hard to find. (Have you seen how unhappy most people are?) For many people in today's world, happiness is an elusive goal. But it isn't for you! That's because you've picked up a book packed with over 300 proven ways to put a smile on your face and help you find your happy.

A lot of people have tips and advice on how to improve your life and find happiness, but only *Happiness Hacks* brings them to you all in one place and in a quick and easy-to-navigate format.

Inside, you'll find a wide variety of happy-inducing ideas, including:

- Put on a Happy Face
- Eat Chocolate
- Say No
- Spend Money on Things
- Flirt with Someone
- Rescue an Animal
- Scream Into a Pillow
- Get the Chip off Your Shoulder

These happiness hacks range from the simple to the grand, but they are all proven to increase your appreciation of life and make you happier.

Flip to any page, and you'll find an idea that will improve your mood and your life!

HACK #1

Decide to Be Happy

This may sound simplistic, but if you want to be happy, then decide to *be* happy. One way to help with this is to think happy thoughts. (That's right, just like Peter Pan told Wendy!) When you choose positive thoughts over negative ones, you are more likely to develop an optimistic outlook on life. Positive people generally have higher levels of optimism and life satisfaction, plus they live longer. And here's some good news—even if you aren't normally a happy person, thinking happy thoughts is a skill you can learn. Work on being an optimist: choose to think positive thoughts and see the proverbial glass as half full rather than half empty. The next time you're driving and someone cuts you off, for example, resist the urge to respond with anger, which can clamp down your blood vessels and increase your blood pressure. Instead, stay positive and let your anger go. Keep that positive vibe going no matter what you're doing. The more frequently you choose to be happy, the happier you will be.

HACK #2

Gaze at a Gorgeous You

Put a picture of yourself from a happy time in your life on your desk. Gaze at an image of yourself looking fabulous. Find a photo of yourself taken when you felt most alive, then frame it and put it where you can easily see it. Looking at positive images of yourself can push aside a mountain of negative thoughts, boost your self-esteem, and make you feel good. What if none of your photos are that great? No problem. Use digital image tools to rework a scanned photo or digital image: erase some of those wrinkles, add some hair, shift some curves, and turn back the clock. Have fun creating a fabulous-looking new you! Then look at the photo whenever you need a little dose of happiness and let it spark some good vibes.

Eat Carbs

This one may seem like a holy grail for carb lovers, but it's true: carbohydrates actually stimulate mood-boosting chemicals in the brain. Carbs promote the production of serotonin, the feel-good brain chemical. Low-carb diets, on the other hand, have been known to cause high levels of anger, tension, and distress. A study that followed people on a low-carbohydrate diet for one year found that those people experienced more depression and anxiety than those on higher-carbohydrate diets. In addition, most whole grains contain fiber, which is good for the heart and the digestive system. So, when that afternoon slump hits, try some healthy, whole-grain/whole-food carbs to get yourself feeling better.

HACK #4

Seduce Someone

Feeling playful and sexy? Slip a little note under your partner's glass and invite him to join you for some fun. Tease, tantalize, and titillate. Let that strap of your little black dress slide off your shoulder. Lean forward and engage your partner's attention. Be seductive. Help your partner believe that in that moment, he is the only person in the world for you. Hold his hand. Let your mutual arousal build and set the pace for everything else. You'll be surprised how happy being sexy makes you feel about yourself and how good it can make your partner feel.

HACK
#5

Schedule Downtime at Work

How do you feel at the end of a typical workday? Are you drained, totally stressed out, or in a bad mood? If so, then you need to get some work happy going on! The best way to do that is to schedule some relaxation time during your workday. We're not talking about taking a two-hour lunch to run to the spa—instead, just find a few moments throughout your day to de-stress and relax. Take a quick cat nap or a half-hour power nap over lunch, step outside for some fresh air and sunlight, go for a brisk walk, do some deep breathing at your desk…all of these are beneficial for banishing stress and helping you refocus. Even if all you can do is sit somewhere for five minutes and close your eyes, you'll be amazed at how much more relaxed and happy you'll feel about your day.

Rescue an Animal

Sadly, not all dogs and cats brought into this world are guaranteed a happy or a long life—just because someone owns an animal does not mean they will properly care for it. Animal shelters all over America often have more animals than they can properly care for, meaning that some animals' lives will end in those shelters. You can make a difference by choosing to adopt a pet from a shelter. Pets bring fun and happiness into your life and have been shown to reduce stress in their owners' lives. So go rescue a friend and make both of your lives better!

HACK #7

Party Like It's Cinco de Mayo

Nothing says happiness like a burrito! Serve beer, beans, and burritos for a Cinco de Mayo party and get into the spirit of Cinco de Mayo, the day that marks the triumph of the Mexican militia over the French army in the 1862 Battle of Puebla. Throw some colorful woven Mexican blankets on the table and set out some green cacti, red chili peppers, and miniature sombreros. Make a centerpiece out of a grouping of candles in terra-cotta pots. Whip up some traditional Mexican foods to go along with your beans and burritos and then serve everything with margaritas and ice-cold Coronas. Invite your neighbors and friends over to eat, drink, and celebrate!

Help Sick Kids

If you are looking to truly make a difference in someone else's life and get a big boatload of happy feelings in return, consider volunteering at a children's hospital or on a hospital's pediatric, neonatal, or nursery wing. You will be making a positive contribution to the lives of sick children and their families, and that's a contribution that can bring meaning to your life too. You'll enjoy knowing that you are helping others—seeing a child smile and knowing that you are responsible for making that smile happen is one of the biggest happiness boosts you can find. Hardworking volunteers are always needed and appreciated by hospital staff, the patients, and their families. When you give friendship and compassion to others in their time of need, happiness flows back to you in abundance.

HACK #9

Don't Be a Hater

Want to feel uplifted and happier? Don't put other people down. Throwing shade at others or participating in malicious gossip will actually rob you of your happiness, so refuse to do it. Don't take part in the mudslinging! If a friend or coworker tries to get you to join in on the negativity, step back, count to ten, and remove yourself from the situation. (Counting is a powerful technique you can use to manage a behavior you want to avoid.) Feel happy knowing that you didn't take part in the bashing, and your friend might see the error of doing so as well. Finding ways to compliment others inspires you to feel happy, whereas gossiping does just the opposite.

HACK
#10

Put on a
Happy Face

Sometimes when it comes to feeling happy, you have to fake it 'til you make it, so force yourself to smile. Now hold that smile for a count of ten. Think to yourself, "I am happy. I am totally, blissfully happy." You'll notice that your mood will begin to shift. You can't help but feel a little lighter. Use your smile to start a happiness epidemic! Smile at everyone, everywhere. People are hardwired to respond to the facial expressions they encounter. If you glower at someone, that person will return a frown, but if you smile, you'll get a smile back. You'll feel happier, too, because your body will respond to your smile even if you are faking the grin. So go ahead—fake it until you genuinely feel happy!

HACK

#11

List Your Top Ten

Millions of people live their lives without a sense of direction. Unless you know what is really important to you and what you want out of life, how are you going to know where you are going or how to get what you want? How will you know what your life's purpose is? Think of ten things that are really important to you. Then make each item as specific as possible. For example, what about your friends especially makes you happy? Is it eating meals together, having people in your life who understand you, or working out tough situations together? Refine the ten things on your list until you know exactly what is of primary importance to you. These are the things that will make you happiest! Knowing what they are can help you make better choices in life.

HACK
#12

Say No

It's easy to say yes—people like you when you say yes to the things they want or need. It's tougher to say no, but sometimes saying no is just the thing you need to feel happier. Is someone trying to push you into doing something you don't have time or the desire to do? Say no. Is someone trying to make you bend on a boundary you feel you need to stand firm on? Say no. Is someone trying to dump a project or task on you? Say no. If you have a hard time saying no, try this: stand in front of a mirror and practice saying, "No, it's not possible," and then turning and walking away. You never again have to give in when you know you don't want to do something or when you know something is not a good idea. Practice until saying no is as easy as saying yes. Saying no is a powerful tool in your game-of-life chest.

HACK #13

Appreciate Your Grandparents

If you grew up with grandparents around, then you are truly lucky. Grandparents are treasure troves of memories and details of a bygone era. They can help you link your life experiences and tribulations to those of your ancestors, giving you a solid feeling about who you are in the grand scheme of life. Grandparents are also great for telling stories about what little troublemakers your parents were as kids. Many people never have that connection to an earlier generation, though, so if you have grandparents, appreciate them now! You'll feel happier in the years to come knowing that you got to spend time with these amazing people and learn from their wisdom.

HACK
#14

Eat Chocolate

When you want a moment of pure pleasure, eat some dark chocolate. Not only does it make you feel good, it has specific health benefits, namely that dark chocolate increases the brain's serotonin and endorphin levels. In other words, it enhances your feelings of pleasure and happiness. Dark chocolate also lowers high blood pressure, improves blood flow through arteries and veins, and acts as a powerful antioxidant. See? Chocolate *is* the perfect food! Just nibbling a little piece of chocolate can lift your spirits.

HACK
#15

Daydream

Have you ever had anyone tell you to "Quit your daydreaming!"? Well, it turns out they were wrong. Daydreaming can stimulate your mind in creative ways, reduce stress, organize your thinking, generate solutions to problems, help you gain new perspectives on troubling issues, and of course, make you feel happier. Assuming that you are not using daydreams to escape from your responsibilities, then regularly daydreaming is not only healthy, it's helpful for solving problems and fostering creativity. Set a timer and let your thoughts take flight to a Greek island, a trekking path high in the Himalayas, a manicured estate in England, a beach in Barbados, or anywhere else you like. Indulge yourself!

HACK #16

Pack Your Pet

Whenever you can steal away for a little rest and relaxation, think about taking your pet with you. Pets bring happiness and love, so why not return the favor and give them a change of scenery and some new experiences? Traveling with a pet has never been easier—many more hotels, campgrounds, and RV parks are becoming pet-friendly. You might find one at your desired vacation destination by searching DogFriendly.com or Pet-friendly-hotels.net or asking other pet owners where they go. If you hesitate to take your dog along on a vacation because he has canine motion sickness, talk with your veterinarian to learn new ways of dealing with that issue. Nondrowsy drugs for motion sickness are available for dogs, for example, or you can take your dog on shorter outings to acclimate him or her to a longer trip.

HACK

#17

Tackle Your Bills

If you are like many people, you hate paying bills, yet deep down you know you have to pay bills to maintain good credit. An excellent way to deal with this unpleasant task is to rip off the proverbial bandage and just tackle the problem. Procrastinating will only increase your stress—relief could be just twenty minutes away. So gather those bills, grab your computer, a calculator, a checkbook, a pen, or whatever you need, and set a timer. Hunker down for twenty minutes or until the job is done. Then reward yourself with a glass of wine, a piece of dark chocolate, or anything that makes you happy.

Go on a Field Trip

Remember the excitement of field trip day when you were a kid—getting to leave school, taking a ride to a new and exciting place, having the thrill of not having to do any work and just having a day full of fun? Do that again! Maybe you have a child in school or a niece or nephew or even a distant cousin. Take a day off work and volunteer to help at an upcoming school-sponsored field trip. Schools are often in need of adult volunteers to accompany children to field trip destinations such as a natural history museum or historic or cultural sites. Not only will you get to see firsthand what your child is experiencing during the field trip and how and what she is being taught, but it is also a lot of fun! As an added benefit, it will also mean a lot to your child that you have taken time off to join her and her classmates. For some kids, that's a really big deal and a source of happiness and pride. Getting to be the cool dad/mom/uncle/aunt is also pretty great!

HACK #19

Scream Into a Pillow

Have you ever been so angry that you felt like you might explode? The next time that happens, scream into a pillow and feel instant relief. This technique releases the pent-up energy that's holding those negative feelings inside—it works especially well when dealing with anger or grief. Scream the words of anger that you can no longer hold in or sob your sorrow into the pillow. Empty out your feelings. Pound the pillow with your fists. You may need to get a bigger pillow or even a new one if your beating destroys it, but that's a small price to pay for getting out your rage. Then, when your peace is restored, do something that makes you happy.

HACK
#20

Make the Most of Your Time in Line

Don't you hate the monotony of having to wait in lines? Well, the next time you are forced to stand in line for something, make a friend! Strike up a conversation with someone you don't know but who looks interesting (and safe). After all, you are both stuck wasting time in line. Why not at least have a nice conversation while you do it? Maybe you have some insight to give, or maybe you can joke about the current in-line-and-waiting situation, or maybe you can just say "Hi!" Others around may join in the conversation; you may meet a group of people who share similar interests (seeing as you're all waiting in the line for the same thing). You never know until you open your mouth and start a conversation. When you're traveling, this is a great way to make friends on the road who can make your traveling experience even more awesome.

Buy a Cup o' Joe for "The Man"

If your boss never notices you, buy her a cup of coffee and that might change. Or just buy your boss coffee as a spontaneous act of thoughtfulness. You may not totally love her, but consider what it might be like to do her job. It is unlikely that your boss was hired because of some kind of likeability quotient—she was probably hired because she had the right credentials, experience, and know-how to do whatever the job entails. If you find your work challenging and stressful at times, imagine what your boss feels. Wouldn't you just love to have someone buy you a cup of coffee when you felt challenged, frustrated, glum, unfocused, behind schedule, or stressed? So buy that cup of coffee for your boss and put a smile on both of your faces.

Ride a Horse

Imagine bundling up in a sweater and scarf on a chilly spring or fall morning and riding horseback along a beach past crashing waves. Or imagine riding through a leafy forest glade, replete with dew-laden spider webs and small critters scurrying out of your path. The world looks and feels different from the back of a horse. Horseback riding seems to heighten your senses of sight, smell, and touch. You'll even get a bit of a workout—riding at a full gallop requires you to use those thigh muscles as well as your feet and hands to stay in the saddle! No matter your pace, the joy you feel seated atop a horse and observing the world is what makes this activity truly worth it.

Throw Your Own Birthday Bash

Instead of having the usual dinner with your significant other or relatives, why not plan a birthday bash that you'll never forget? Perhaps you want to fly to London to shop at Harrods and then go to the theater district to see a play. What are you waiting for? Book the trip. You only live once. Or maybe you've always wanted to go mountain climbing or scuba diving or skydiving. Get on the Internet, find out what's involved, and do it. Whatever you do, do it your way and enjoy every minute of it.

HACK
#24

Donate Your Couch Coins

For a quick dose of happiness, gather up that loose change in the cushions of your couch or lying around the house and give it to a good cause. By some estimates, the average American household has as much as $90 lying under sofa cushions, in dresser drawers, and even in the laundry room (where a lot of it comes out in the wash). There are myriad ways to donate your loose change: drop the coins into charity boxes at grocery store checkout lines, give it to your church or temple, or simply donate it to your favorite charitable organization. Happiness researchers say that when you perform selfless acts of generosity for others, you increase your happiness.

Tell Someone You're Proud of Them

The statement "I am proud of you!" is something people don't hear very often, yet hearing it does so much for the recipient's self-esteem. Be generous with your encouragement and praise! It costs you nothing and can mean happiness for those who hear it. Through your example, you can show others that happiness isn't necessarily being successful at work, having lots of money, or having the latest car model in your garage.

Fix a Fault

Everyone has faults, but that doesn't mean you are stuck with yours. Pick a fault you would like to change or eliminate. First, be completely honest with yourself and examine what faults you have. Are you a gossip? Do you have a quick temper and a short fuse? Do you procrastinate and avoid facing problems until they've snowballed out of control? Are you still blaming others for the things that are wrong with your life? Choose to fix what you don't like about yourself. See goodness in yourself and others.

Have a Sushi Party

Sharing a meal with friends is one of the most pleasurable activities known to humankind, so why not invite some friends over and make your own food? Host a hands-on sushi-making party. Tell each person to invite someone else too. You get the supplies (sushi rice, nori or seaweed sheets, crab, cucumber, avocado, and other fillings). Explain the directions: each person puts the rice on a strip of nori, adds the desired filling, rolls the sheet, wets one end and wraps it over the other to seal it closed, and then cuts the roll into several pieces. Then everyone can share their creations, talk, laugh, and eat together. Sake, anyone?

HACK

#28

Feed Your Brain

Like the old saying goes, you are what you eat. If you want to be happier, then you better start eating some good-for-you food! Junk food will weigh you down and depress your moods, whereas healthier foods will improve your body and brain health and lead to you feeling happier and more energized. Omega-3 fatty acids are especially good for your brain health and are necessary for survival, yet your body doesn't produce them. You need to get them in the foods you eat, such as in fish like halibut, herring, salmon, sardines, snapper, swordfish, and tuna. Other good sources of omega-3 fatty acids are flaxseed and walnuts, wheat germ, pumpkin, and spinach. If you want a healthy heart and you want food for your brain, eat your omega-3s.

HACK #29

Imagine Fame

Sure, your work is pretty satisfying, but you still want recognition for those big accomplishments and milestones. Draw the fame you desire by using the law of attraction. Before you retire for the night, take five minutes to clear your mind. Focus. Use your imagination to create a scenario in which you are receiving accolades, praise, and ovations. Now add emotions to your imagined scene. Concentrate on your feelings and mood as you listen to the words others are saying about your achievements. Your subconscious doesn't know real experiences from imagined ones—according to the law of attraction, you just have to believe the experience can be yours and then supercharge it with emotion in order for it to manifest in your life. Let those happy feelings permeate your dreams and your subsequent time at work.

HACK #30

Think of Two Ways Life Could Be Better

Your boyfriend walks out on you. Your dog dies. Your new car is totaled by a tree limb. Your boss announces layoffs and your name is on the list. Some days, it seems that nothing goes right. But change is certain, and things can and do get better. Think of two ways your life could change in positive ways! A new partner walks into your life…with dogs. Your new job comes with a car. Life is good and you are on top of the world. Relish the thought!

HACK #31

Pack Less

Lugging a big suitcase around wherever you go can cause more than one kind of headache—for one thing, most airlines now charge a fee to handle checked bags. Traveling light makes more sense than ever! Purchase basic travel clothing that is lightweight, wrinkle free, and washable, in neutral colors like black and tan that can be dressed up easily for any fancy occasions during your trip. Pack less, travel light, and avoid the headaches.

HACK #32

Get More Friends

According to happiness research, friendships have a bigger effect on your happiness than your income does. Companionship stimulates your brain's attachment and social group circuitry, both of which help you feel safe and loved. According to a survey by the National Opinion Research Center, on average, the more friends you have, the happier you are. Furthermore, friendship itself lights up your brain in all the right areas. In October 2010, researchers at Harvard University found that brain areas associated with calm, familiarity, and happiness would respond more strongly when people were thinking about a friend versus a stranger with similar interests (such as a work colleague). If you can't see your friends, at least think about them.

Be Grateful

When you focus on what you love about your life, your positive emotional brain fires up. This creates a focused, positive feeling free of worry and fear, a state of mind that allows you to truly enjoy moments of happiness. Before you go to sleep each night, write down at least five things you're grateful for and pause to re-experience the pleasure each one brings you. Focus on what is making you feel lucky and good about your life, and you will soon find that you feel more positive in general and that you begin to slow down and savor the good times.

Have an Orgasm

It doesn't take a genius to know that sex can make you happy. For most people, having sex creates pleasurable feelings that (hopefully) lead to orgasm. An orgasm provides the biggest blast of legal, naturally occurring dopamine available to your brain. After scanning the brains of lucky volunteers who were experiencing orgasms at the time, Dutch researchers likened their brain scans to scans of people experiencing heroin rushes!

Slow It Down

Learn the art of savoring something: choose a pleasurable experience and slow it down. Let's say you're taking a walk. Along the way, stop in your tracks and slowly take in a panoramic view of your surroundings. Pause to smell a flower or pet your neighbor's dog. Stop occasionally to slowly breathe in the fresh air and feel it replenishing your lungs. Allow the scents of the season to revive memories of happy days in your past. Or spend a half hour truly listening to your favorite music, lingering in a bath, or massaging your partner. The point is to luxuriate in whatever activity brings you physical, mental, and emotional pleasure.

HACK #36

Sleep More

If you want to have a good attitude and feel happier about your life, then make sure you get good sleep. Your body needs it! Without sufficient sleep, sleep researchers say, your mental function becomes impaired: for example, insufficient sleep can negatively impact your daytime performance, causing lower levels of energy and duller thinking. Inadequate sleep has serious consequences. Certain regulatory systems and important organs continue their vital work while you sleep—in fact, researchers have been able to pinpoint parts of the brain that actually increase their activities when subjects are asleep. Getting adequate sleep enables you to wake up refreshed, energized, and in a good mood.

HACK
#37

Go on Vacation

Take your vacation days—they're good for you! One study found that the risk of suffering a fatal heart attack decreased in middle-aged men who regularly took an annual vacation. Even so, roughly a third of Americans who have accrued vacation time don't take all the time they are allotted. Vacations can restore the balance between work and the other areas of your life by providing relief from the relentless pressures of work commitments, schedules, and deadlines. Even if you don't travel anywhere, take some vacation days to just hang out, sleep, and rejuvenate yourself. Then you can return to work feeling happy and recharged.

HACK

#38

Get the Chip Off Your Shoulder

If you want to be happy, then don't harbor a grudge. Holding on to anger, resentment, and hostility hurts you, psychologically, emotionally, and physically. Even if the incident happened only yesterday, the person you are mad at may not even remember the incident, so what's the point in continuing to be angry? Don't give up your power to have positivity in your life just to harbor a grudge. Find a way to move past it. Take an anger management class or read books offering specific strategies for dealing with anger issues. Take good care of yourself—love and respect yourself enough to let go of a grudge.

Tell a (Funny) Joke

Telling a funny joke is a terrific way to cheer up others, defuse tense situations, add levity in times of stress. The key here is to make a funny joke, not something overly corny or lame. Memorizing a joke and telling it to others is a good way to cultivate a sense of humor. Plus, did you know that laughing may actually reduce your risk for heart disease? Laughing can also mitigate the damage that's incurred when you are experiencing deep distress and pain. Want to feel good? Be able to laugh at stressful situations.

Eat Your Favorite Food

You know how happy you feel when you're eating your favorite food. That's why it's your favorite. Cook or order that one dish that just puts a smile on your face. It could be comfort food from your childhood, an exotic creation you first tasted on vacation, or even a savory palate-pleaser you learned to cook when you were dating someone from another country. Happily savor every bite of that Moroccan tagine chicken, New England crab cake, Midwestern meatloaf, Southern fried chicken, or whatever is your favorite.

HACK

#41

Feel the Luck of the Bamboo

Put a "lucky bamboo" plant on your kitchen counter, where it will happily enjoy some warmth. Even if you don't have a green thumb, you can successfully grow this plant. It doesn't need much light and will thrive in plain old water (as long as the water is clean and kept at the same level in the vase or jar). According to the ancient Chinese tradition of feng shui, the "lucky bamboo"—actually not a bamboo at all, but a member of the *Dracaena* family—creates harmony wherever it is placed. Its numerous long green leaves gracefully grow out of slender stalks. Put a three-stalk plant in the bedroom to ensure longevity, wealth, and happiness, or if you work from home, put a six-stalk plant in your office to attract prosperity.

Get Thee to a Church/Synagogue/ Service

Attend at least one service in your spiritual faith this week. Research suggests that participation and belief in a religious faith or spiritual tradition is an important ingredient in a purposeful, self-actualized, meaningful, and happy life. One way to stay in touch with your core spiritual beliefs is to attend a religious service or gathering where others share your faith and beliefs. Some studies link regular participation in such events to a greater sense of well-being, a stronger connection to community, a reinforcement of personal beliefs, and a more stable, healthy, and happy family life. If you don't have a specific faith, create a regular ritual to honor what you believe in. It can be an elaborate affair, or it can be something as simple as finding a few minutes to read about or reflect upon beliefs that inspire you.

HACK #43

Take Your Partner on Vacation

Nothing thrives through neglect. This is especially true for romantic relationships. Lavish the kind of attention on your romantic partner that you desire for yourself! Make a reservation at one of the best hotels or bed-and-breakfast establishments in your area. Such accommodations usually offer intimate, cozy settings and comfortable bedrooms (sometimes with fireplaces and Jacuzzi tubs). Surprise your partner with a weekend getaway and watch how your love blossoms.

Practice Random Kindness

Push the button in the elevator for a fellow rider. Help an elderly person up the steps of a building or a subway exit or onto a bus. Put your pocket change into a charity box. Invite a fellow shopper to move ahead of you in the check-out line. Shovel the snow off your neighbor's walk. Offer to let someone share your umbrella. Random acts of kindness require very little effort, but such acts pay great dividends in the good karma and personal happiness they generate.

Donate Blood

The greatest gift you can give anyone is the gift of life. Hospitals nationwide provide lifesaving blood transfusions every day, yet all too often a shortage of blood prompts blood donation centers, the American Red Cross, and hospitals to call upon citizens to donate. Consider donating on a regular basis or even just once a year—perhaps make your donation on your birthday so that someone else can make it to his or her next birthday. The happiness you feel on your special day will be magnified by your generosity.

Flirt with Someone

Flirting is fun and harmless and can make you feel good about yourself.
Next time you're in a bookshop or coffee shop—or even a supermarket!—
try a little flirting. Let's say you see a great-looking guy thumbing through
a travel guide. Or maybe an attractive woman is standing in front of the sci-
ence fiction novels or shelves of business books. The point is that you like
what you see. You could walk over, excuse yourself, and reach past her to
retrieve a book that's right in front of her. If you're a bit timid, simply flash
a nice smile after making eye contact. Or comment on the travel book he's
reading. Is it a guide to Ireland, where you once bicycled through rolling
hills? Have you read *Finnegans Wake*? Show your curiosity and interest in
the topic (and the person) and get your best flirt on.

HACK
#47

Tell Someone Else to Cook

Ever too tired to cook? Feel like having to plan what's for dinner is the bane of your existence? Don't let that stress you out and rob your happiness. Encourage (or tell) each family member to choose one day each week to prepare dinner. Be graceful and supportive if you're presented with a stack of peanut butter and jelly sandwiches—at least you didn't have to make them! If you have children, get them an age-appropriate cookbook and help them make some recipes. After that, they're on their own. Train the whole family so that the next time you are too tired to cook, you can relax and check the family schedule to see whose turn it is to cook instead.

Make a Birthday Card

Making a card that says exactly what you want to say is way more fun than perusing dozens of cards on a store shelf. Oh, and since it costs nothing when you already have the materials on hand, you've got another reason to smile! A sheet or two of colored paper, paste, scissors, colored pens, and some magazines are all you need to make a great, personalized birthday card guaranteed to evoke smiles of appreciation. Find birthday greetings on the Internet or make up your own, then use magazines to clip out images or words that express your thoughts. Have fun with it! You'll find that the receiver of the card will be far more appreciative of all your hard work than if you had simply pulled a generic card off a shelf.

Grow Your Own Veggies

Freshly picked vegetables taste far superior to and have greater nutritional value than their shipped-and-warehoused counterparts. Why not make your body healthier and yourself happier by growing your own vegetables? Plant a small garden and include companion plantings—plants that repel specific pests next to plants that would otherwise attract those pests—to naturally minimize the pest population. You don't need much space for a small garden, but if space is a major consideration, you can grow your veggies in pots and planters on the patio instead of in a garden bed. As an added healthy bonus, you will also be certain your veggies haven't been treated with chemical fertilizers or pesticides.

HACK #50

Take a Spa Day

When you feel like life has become a treadmill and you just need to step off, treat yourself to a day at the spa. Get a manicure, a pedicure, or a skin rejuvenation facial. If you'd like to try something a tad more radical, get a colon cleansing, take a mud bath, or slip into a sensory-deprivation tank. For a healthy state of mind and body, try some treatments at an upscale med-spa center that integrates innovative, cutting-edge therapies and holistic wellness modalities with the ancient healing practices of other cultures.

Relax Before Bed

After a long day at work, are you tense? Are you tossing and turning while trying to go to sleep every night? If you release your stress before you go to bed, you may find you are able to fall asleep more quickly, have a better quality of sleep, and wake up more rested and refreshed. There are lots of ways to calm your mind and let go of the tension you hold in your body, including taking a warm bath, sipping a glass of wine, listening to peaceful music, doing some deep breathing, or praying to release your concerns to a higher power. Rather than living a stressed-out life, make a point to let go of the tension you've accumulated throughout the day so that you get deep, restorative sleep.

Make a Budget (and Stick to It)

When most people think "make a budget," they don't relate budgeting with being happy. But if you are living in debt (which is not very happy), then making a budget is your ticket onto the happy train. When you know where you are going, you can control how you get there! Start by writing down exactly how much money you have coming in each month and the sources of your income streams. List all your bills, starting with those that carry late payment fees or debts that come with high interest rates. Make another list of your monthly needs. Brainstorm low-cost ways to meet your financial obligations and needs: making your lunch instead of buying it, taking a thermos of coffee to work with you and forgoing your usual cup at the local coffee house, carpooling instead of driving solo. Write the due dates of all bills on your calendar. Live frugally, but feel empowered as little by little you watch your debt begin to shrink and your savings begin to grow.

HACK
#53

Carry a Bag for Someone

Come to the aid of someone struggling with her luggage. Maybe she's trying to get onto the tram that goes to the airport and you are going her way, or perhaps your traveling buddy is headed back from the local flea market and his rented bike is overloaded with bags. You could take one and lighten his load. Or maybe you see a senior crossing the street after buying her groceries and she's struggling with her bags. Don't wait for someone else to rush over and help her—do so yourself. And put a smile on your face. Everyone needs a helping hand sometimes!

Bake Cookies for the Office Grouch

If someone in your office often scowls, chronically complains, or flies into fits with little or no provocation, offer him a plate of warm cookies. Even if your cookies are refused, you can be assured that you at least tried to bring a little pleasure into that person's life. This gesture may work...or it may not. Some people get so used to being unhappy and feeling like the whole world is against them that they are outside of their comfort zone when someone does do something unexpected and nice for them. The truth is that the grouch is probably hungry for friendship and attention.

Tell the Truth, the Whole Truth, and Nothing but the Truth

Can you go through an entire day telling the truth and only the truth? Telling the truth, like thinking positive thoughts, is a skill that requires lots of practice. People tell little white lies, half-truths, or useful falsehoods for all kinds of reasons: to evade blame, deceive, deny reality, or feel better about themselves. In some instances, a little white lie might be motivated by a desire to prevent someone from being hurt. For example, you know that a coworker is about to be fired, but when he asks you if you've heard anything about his possible termination, you tell him no. It takes more effort to think about how to answer him truthfully and still not hurt his feelings than to just lie. But if you live and work from a place of truth, others will trust your word and will appreciate your honesty.

HACK #56

Write a Thank-You Note

A member of your work team helped you meet a deadline, someone stood in for you in a meeting, your partner took on part of your housework, your parent baked you your favorite meal… Whatever the kindness was, take the time to write that person a thank-you note. And don't send the thank-you note by email! A handwritten thank-you note is a much more personal expression of appreciation. When you let people know that you view them and their contributions as important and meaningful by taking the time to write a thoughtful note, most likely you'll be rewarded with loyalty and assistance the next time you need help.

Dance Around the Kitchen

Start your day with a little salsa, mambo, cha-cha-cha, or your favorite dance steps as you make your way over to measure the coffee, add the water, and turn on the pot. Dance until the coffee is ready. Have a cup and then dance some more! Start your fancy footwork in your kitchen and jig throughout your house. If you have to leave for work, dance your way to your dressing room and keep moving while you do your makeup. Dance over to pick up your purse, briefcase, and car keys…and then dance right into the garage. Keep moving and feel your smiles emerge and pounds melt away.

Collect Something

One of the easiest ways to start a collection is by acquiring something that attracts you, perhaps because of its historical significance, beauty, or value. Whether it's amber jewelry, classic toys from your childhood, salt and pepper sets from the turn of the century, old comic books, or whatever else that captures your fancy, use that piece to start a collection. Set a budget for your collection and make space in your home for it. Expand what you know about your collectibles and network with others who buy and sell those items. And then spend many happy hours searching for items to add to your collection!

Have Coffee with an Adversary

Rather than letting resentment grow and ruin your happiness, find a way to work with an adversary. Say you owned a vintage dress shop four doors down from another secondhand dress store that just opened. Would you sit down and meet with the new owner if the knowledge you gained from the meeting would help you both compete better? That might be a good idea, right? Suggest having coffee as a way to open dialogue between you and your "adversary." Use the time to see where your two ideologies dovetail and where they depart. Actively listen and repeat aloud what you think you just heard. You may discover discrepancies between what was actually said and what you thought was said. See if you can find common ground. Is there a way you might team up to bring more business into both stores? Find win-win scenarios that might serve you both well.

HACK
#60

Make Fido Some Food

Nothing makes you feel happier than the love and appreciation of your dog. That tail wagging in joy is a great smile-inducer! So treat your best friend well by keeping him healthy. Instead of buying dog biscuits or other doggie treats, consider making some healthy homemade treats. Look for recipes on the Internet or make up your own using natural ingredients (just be sure to first look up what dogs can and cannot eat). Just like humans, dogs like foods that taste good. Remember to avoid no-no foods like chocolate, onions, and grapes, as well as artificial ingredients and additives that might cause illness (or even be deadly) for some dogs. You'll feel better knowing that your dog is healthy and happy.

HACK #61

Pat Your Own Back

You praise your friends, your coworkers, and your spouse whenever they accomplish something praiseworthy, so why not give yourself some praise? You're not being a braggart or egotistical when you acknowledge that you finished a task or made a breakthrough—you work very hard and accomplish many things that no one but you ever recognizes. If you finally played a complicated piano composition all the way through or found an ingenious way to increase your project's budget, tell yourself how wonderfully brilliant and accomplished you are. Bask in the glory of the moment! You deserve it.

HACK #62

Drink Wine with Friends

If you and your friends enjoy wine, consider forming a wine club. (A club where you get to drink is one of the best kinds!) Host monthly meetings where you have blind tastings. Here's how you do it. First, before each meeting, decide on one type of wine you will taste that session: Pinot (Noir or Gris), Cabernet Sauvignon, Burgundy, Chardonnay, Sauvignon Blanc, Zinfandel, or whatever you like. Have each person bring a bottle of the selected type of wine and one appetizer to share with everyone. (If you're going to be drinking all that wine, you'll want some food in your stomach too!) Wrap each bottle in a numbered paper bag so that no one can see the label (and possibly form a bias), then give everyone pencils and notecards and have them write down their comments about each bottle they taste. Let the adventure begin! You may discover a new favorite wine. At the very least, you'll have a great time trying something new with your friends.

Experiment with Essential Oils

Essential oils are distillations of plants that have beneficial properties. Some are stimulating; some are calming. You can find a large number of relaxing aromatic oils on the market, but the most popular include lavender, sage, sandalwood, frankincense, and chamomile. How you use them is up to you. Some people light scented candles as they relax after a hard day's work; others prefer to place a few drops of scented oil in their bathwater or on their pillow to help them unwind and fall asleep faster at night. The important thing is to select a fragrance that is both appealing and relaxing. Floral scents tend to work best, because food scents can make you hungry. Avoid tart or biting fragrances, such as lemon, because they may have the opposite effect, perking you up instead of calming you down. You may have to experiment until you find the scent that is right for you, but it is definitely worth the effort.

Learn CPR and Be a Hero

How exactly will learning CPR bring you happiness? Imagine the happiness you would feel if you were personally able to save someone's life. You can prepare by learning some simple first-aid techniques, cardiopulmonary resuscitation (CPR), and the Heimlich maneuver. Classes are offered through the American Heart Association, parks and recreation departments in many cities, and also through local hospitals and clinics as part of community outreach programs. Find and take a class near you. Then, if you witness someone having a medical emergency, you can apply what you have learned. You may even save someone's life through your quick actions. Now *that's* something to be truly happy about!

Stretch

You know how stiff your body feels when you finally get out of a chair after hours of crunching numbers or going through email? Fortunately, it only takes a few minutes to stretch. Some stretches can even be done while sitting in a chair or standing in front of your desk. If you happen to have a yoga mat, take it with you on your break or your lunch hour to a private, peaceful area and do some stretches. You'll feel rejuvenated, flexible, centered, and happier.

Look for the Good in a Bad Situation

Everyone of us has experienced losses—some more extreme than others—but there is often a seed of triumph hidden in those losses. It may be hard to see at first, but it's there. Try asking yourself: "What is the good in this? What lesson can I take away? How can I share my knowledge with others?" Bring to mind two or three events that may have seemed totally awful up to this point and write down only the good things and/or the benefits gained from each. Looking for the brighter side is a great habit to develop—you'll become a happier and more compassionate person.

HACK

#67

Bring Your Pillow

Lack of sleep often makes people miserable, so hedge your bet when you are traveling and bring your favorite pillow with you. Pillows generally stuff easily into a carry-on bag and can serve as a terrific insurance policy against sleepless nights. Traveling can sap your energy by various means, including jet lag, but one of the best ways to regain that lost energy is to get plenty of rest. When traveling on a business trip or a family vacation, the pillows in your hotel room (or on a cruise ship or train) may not be great, but you can always pull out your favorite pillow and know that blissful sleep is only moments away.

Admit That You Screwed Up

It's often difficult to admit that you made a mistake, especially to your superiors at work. However, doing so demonstrates your sense of responsibility and your willingness to shoulder blame. Taking responsibility for a screwup by you or your team shows your managers and bosses that you are a person with values and moral principles. Although a mistake has been made, you'll be better off admitting it and moving forward than deceiving, lying, or covering up the error, all of which can have disastrous consequences for you later, when others finally find out the truth.

HACK

#69

Spend Money on Things

That's right, spending money can make you happy—as long as you spend money on *doing* things and not on *stuff*. Spend your hard-earned cash on pleasurable or enlightening experiences like concerts, vacations, trips to art museums, cooking classes, yoga workshops, or a night out with friends. Participating in experiences has been shown to provide more long-lasting happiness than buying things. Spending money on other people (such as family and friends) is a great way to boost your happiness levels...and get out there and have fun with the ones you love. Truly enjoying pleasant life experiences allows you to "smell the roses" and train your brain to more fully experience higher levels of zest and happiness.

Anticipate More

Anticipation is often sweeter than the actual experience, particularly when the upcoming event is guaranteed to be pleasurable, such as going out on a romantic date or taking a beach vacation. Anticipating future rewards lights up the pleasure centers in your brain in the same way that experiencing the event does. Think about it: you feel butterflies and grin endlessly an hour before that special date. That's because your brain recognizes all of the pleasant situations leading up to the ultimate reward. So dream up something that will lead to joyful anticipation! Even if making it happen seems an impossibility, envision what you'd like to happen in minute detail and savor each mental picture. Remember, intensely visualizing something can trick your brain into thinking it's an actual experience. It really is almost like being there.

Eat Some Turkey (Gobble, Gobble)

We all love Thanksgiving for the release of serotonin that comes from eating turkey, which is loaded with tryptophan. Extra tryptophan in your diet leads to extra serotonin in your brain, which is why tryptophan supplements are touted as a sleep aid and mood lifter (among other things). Foods that provide tryptophan include roasted white turkey, ground beef, cottage cheese, chicken thighs, eggnog, milk, and almonds.

HACK

#72

Say Hi to the Person Next to You

Pay attention to the people around you. Instead of silently standing next to a stranger for an elevator ride up several floors, look her in the eyes and offer a greeting. "Hello!" is easy to say. It's only one word. It might lead into a conversation about the weather, the latest news about your city or town, or something about the surroundings (the noise next door due to construction, for example). You'll never know where elevator chitchat might lead if you don't open your mouth in the first place. That stranger could become a new friend or romantic interest!

HACK

#73

Get a Bestie Massage

Let your best friend know how much you value her friendship by inviting her along for a relaxing afternoon at the spa. Treat her to her favorite relaxation treatment or a hot stone massage. Imagine how great she'll feel when the massage therapist places warm stones of smooth volcanic rock on her tired back, shoulders, and neck muscles. If there's been any friction between you, a spa day can ease that as well. Go ahead and book that appointment! Invest some time and cost in your friendship—a happy relationship with your best friend is worth every penny.

HACK
#74

Have Cash on You

Always keep some cash on hand, even if it's only a small amount. Not only can cash help in an emergency situation, there's something reassuring about having money in your purse or pocket. You're never broke or helpless as long as you have cash. Not only can that money help you feel secure, but it also can work as a mental boost. Imagine that money attracting more money into your life. Positive and hopeful thinking and dreaming can get you started, goals will pull you a little further along, and creative ingenuity and concrete effort will remove obstacles and shift a flow of money into your life.

Turn on the Juice

During a crisis, your body releases turbocharged stress hormones that flood into your cardiovascular system to prepare you to deal with the emergency at hand. Unfortunately, stress hormones flooding the system can also cause damage. Antioxidants—which are beneficial natural chemicals found in high levels in certain foods—act as scavengers of free radicals, the by-products that are created when cells use oxygen. Antioxidants can both prevent and repair damage caused by free radicals. Squeeze or use a juicer to extract the juice from organic fruits and vegetables such as oranges, limes, strawberries, apricots, peaches, cantaloupes, carrots, and green leafy vegetables. Pomegranate, purple grapes, and cranberries are high in phytochemicals and antioxidants as well. Drinking fresh, organic juice is especially beneficial when you are under duress.

Help Someone Who Is Lost

Nothing is more frustrating (and in some cases more frightening) than being lost in a new city or unfamiliar place. Be the person you would like to meet if you were lost! If you notice a distressed visitor trying to figure out a map in an area you know well, offer to help him. Point him in the right direction. When you give directions, write them down and carefully explain the distances, turns, and notable landmarks. Communicate as clearly as possible. Who knows? Your kindness may one day inspire that same distressed traveler to help another person in the same way.

HACK #77

Give a Great Tip

No one enjoys picking up dirty, wet towels or cleaning sinks and showers of soap scum, whiskers, and hair. Housekeepers and motel workers make very little money, yet their work—in addition to being tedious and dirty—is often thankless. Your generous tip will help them better provide for their families and tell them that you appreciated their work. And you can feel happier knowing that you brightened someone's day.

HACK
#78

See Yourself Reaching Your Goal

What's your primary personal goal? Is it to lose weight, spend less, or earn more money? Whatever it is, write out an affirmation for achieving it. For example: "From now on at mealtimes, I will eat one-third less" or "I will walk for a half hour each day." Try to keep your affirmation succinct and to the point. That way, it will be easy to recall and repeat at least three times during the day. The more specific your affirmation, the more effective it will be in helping you attain your goal.

Be On Time for Meetings

Although many company meetings may seem dull and mundane, it says a lot about you and your work ethic if you show up on time and prepared for them. This in turn will make your coworkers look at your favorably, which of course will lead to increased work happiness. Whether you are leading a meeting or simply attending a meeting, if you are expected to provide input, ideas, or data, take time to prepare yourself. Being prepared and on time demonstrates a high level of integrity and commitment. Be proud of yourself for making the effort.

Do Yoga with a Friend

Exercise can make you happier, but sometimes it can be a drag. One way to motivate yourself to exercise is to do it with a friend, so invite a friend to be your exercise buddy! Walk together during your lunch hour. Ride bikes or rollerblade around a local park. Take an aerobics swimming class. Do yoga together. The point is to make exercise fun—make it a social event as much as it is a workout. When you're laughing and conversing, the time goes by much more quickly. Socializing stimulates the mind just as exercise increases blood flow. Both nourish you and should be part of a healthy lifestyle.

Trick Your Brain Into Happiness

There's a way you can "trick" your mind into reliving a happy event *as if it is actually happening again*. Simply draw a picture in your mind of a past happy event. Use sensory details to make it come alive in your mind, creating a tangible feeling of happy anticipation. Now slowly bring yourself back to the present by becoming re-centered in your body, from the soles of your feet to the crown of your head. Take a deep breath and slowly open your eyes. You will likely feel rejuvenated and happy, ready to focus on thinking happy thoughts. This process can spark existing neurons and strengthen neural connections associated with the original memory, essentially doubling your levels of pleasure and happiness. The more you remember happy times, the happier your outlook on life will become.

Paint the Places You Go

If you like to dabble with art (even if you aren't very good at it), take some paint with you on your next vacation, then paint a scene somewhere during your trip. It doesn't have to be ornate or perfect—just the quiet, still activity of painting will help you feel relaxed and centered. And there's a bonus: when you get home from your sojourns into the world, you'll feel happy looking at your paintings and remembering the good times you had on your trip and the places you visited.

HACK #83

Convince Yourself to Be Positive

Perhaps you are nervous about an upcoming situation, and your mind keeps going over all the things that could go wrong. Instead of letting a barrage of negative thoughts take over your life, create a list of positive affirmations to counter them. Suppose you are nervous about going to a party where you will know no one except the hostess, who will obviously be very busy. Repeating a positive phrase like "I will be relaxed, sociable, and have a really fun time" fifty times a day every day before the party (in five sets of ten) will create an expectation in your mind that your brain will be happy to fulfill.

HACK #84

Pet Sit

Cleaning up poop may not immediately seem like the path to happiness, but helping a friend and their furry (or scaly or feathered) friend is. Pet sitting is also a great way to decide on whether or not you would want a pet. It's a good idea to care for the animal in its own environment rather than in your home—a puppy that likes to chew on things, for example, may ruin your favorite book or your shoes. You can learn a lot from pet sitting. You might discover that a guinea pig is not the right pet for you because of its nocturnal nature, for instance. An iguana might not be active enough, and a parrot might be too possessive or too talkative. But if you connect with your friend's pet, there's a good chance you'll enjoy your pet sitting experience. Discover what many pet owners have learned: pets bring much fun and happiness!

HACK
#85

Hold an Oscars Party

Looking for an excuse to break the monotony of your winter doldrums? Get into the party spirit and host an Oscars bash! Since film buffs say that Hollywood films were in their heyday in the 1930s and 1940s, ask everyone to dress in attire that reflects those golden decades of filmmaking. Offer appetizers and drinks and pass around cards asking your guests to pick the nominees for Best Actress, Best Actor, Best Screenplay, and Best Picture… and then enjoy the Oscars and cheer on your picks.

HACK #86

Do a Mini-Meditation

Feeling stressed, overwhelmed, and decidedly unhappy? Try cooling down with a mini-meditation: stop whatever you are doing right now, close your eyes, and focus on your breath until your mind quiets. As thoughts come up, allow them to float away by, gently redirecting your mind back to your inhalations and exhalations, blotting out whatever is going on around you. Stay in your mini-meditation for fifteen minutes (or start with five minutes and work your way up to fifteen minutes). With practice, you can easily learn to quiet any mind chatter that may be distracting you. Doing a mini-meditation is a great way to refocus yourself and find some calm.

Stand Up to Politics

Are you dissatisfied with politicians? Do you hope for change? Do you hold a brighter vision for America and the world? Mahatma Gandhi once advised people to be the change they want to see in the world. That means get off the couch, get away from television, and go out into the world and do something to bring about that change. Join with others who share your passion about creating a more meaningful life and a better future through political action. Living and working toward a more meaningful and purpose-driven life is an important part of achieving happiness.

Keep Your Promises

One way to spread happiness is to keep your promises. Just as you see someone who is faithful to their word as a trustworthy person, your friends, family, and business colleagues will also trust you when you keep your promises. In this age of spin, when facts get altered in ways to deliberately mislead people and to further ideological agendas, let your truth be absolute and do what you say you'll do. It isn't always easy to align feelings, thoughts, beliefs, and spoken words so that no one questions your truthfulness or integrity, but keeping your promises will put you on the path to being that trustworthy person others can depend on.

HACK
#89

Inspire Someone

Your personal stories can inspire someone to achieve success! You can also inspire someone to believe in herself, overcome adversity, or just feel a little happier when her mood is dark. Comforting someone who's lost, alone, or sad is a way of spreading happiness. You can help someone replace the negative energy in her life with positive energy. Sharing personal stories can help people who have lost hope regain control of their lives and begin to search for answers to their own problems or find new meaning in their lives. Let your stories help others appreciate their own positive qualities.

Make the World Better

Think of three things you can do that don't cost money but can benefit the world and the people around you. You could pick up trash along your daily walk, for example, or you could plant a tree or two. Recycle, if you don't already. Hold open a door for a mother with a small child in a stroller. Give a construction worker or roofer a fresh bottle of water while he's working up a sweat. Implement as many of these make-the-world-better ideas as you can! You'll feel the joy of knowing that you are truly making the world a better place one selfless action at a time.

HACK
#91

Notice the Wonders of Life

Incredible things are happening all around you all the time! Just for a moment, notice the wonders of life: look at the way light shimmers on dew drops clinging to an elaborate spider's web, smell the scent of lilacs after a hard rain, watch the majestic flight of eagles, savor the taste of a freshly cut watermelon, gaze at the pattern of a piece of gum stuck to the pavement, admire the vibrant color of a peacock feather, hear the sizzle of a marshmallow toasted over a crackling fire. Noticing life's little details will fire up your imagination and your natural inquisitiveness about the world.

Get Stuck

Acupuncture, a traditional Chinese medicine, is the process of inserting slender needles slightly under the skin at various points in the body in order to balance the flow of energy (chi) throughout the body. Whether you believe in the literal existence of chi or not, acupuncture can help you feel healthier and happier. Researchers have found that acupuncture can benefit people who are experiencing depression, anxiety, and other problems, including insomnia. Some researchers believe that your brain releases neurotransmitters (happy juice) in reaction to the needles, although there isn't complete agreement on how acupuncture works. One study showed that people who had acupuncture had less anxiety and a better memory afterward, compared to a control group that didn't undergo acupuncture. And for mood disorders, acupuncture can work immediately, unlike prescription drugs or talk therapy, and it has few side effects (except for that pesky needles-hurt-going-in part).

Acupuncture is one of those treatments where "Don't try this at home!" applies. Instead, seek out a licensed acupuncturist (licensing varies from state to state).

HACK #93

Stay in Touch with Friends You Meet on Vacation

Nothing brings back memories of a trip like receiving mail from friends you made while on vacation. If they don't know how to contact you once you've left, though, you won't be getting the piece of art they promised to send, their postcards, or their letters, so don't forget to exchange your addresses (snail mail and email both) with new friends you meet and make while traveling. You'll enjoy memories of that trip all over again when they contact you. If you're lucky, you might even be invited back!

HACK #94

No Smoking!

Want to feel healthier, happier, and even a little richer? Quit smoking! In addition to saving your life, you'll also be saving some cash—if you give up a three-packs-a-day habit, you'll save thousands of dollars each year. Besides, nicotine addiction can wreak havoc on your health, and your medical bills will cost you more than your smokes will. Quitting will help you live longer and feel happier about yourself and your life. If you want to quit but haven't been successful, don't give up! Many ex-smokers had to quit several times before they were successful. There are lots of ways to quit. If at first you don't succeed, don't forget to talk to your doctor about getting help.

HACK #95

Create New Ways to Make Money

Perhaps you are one of those craftsy people who enjoy beadwork and like to make earrings, belt buckles, or pins while watching television at night. Maybe you have a passion for sports collectibles and like to pour over your collectibles in your leisure time. Whatever your interest, passion, or hobby, consider how you could turn it into income. Could you make something to sell at local art and wine festivals, on *eBay*, on *Etsy*, or in galleries that feature the work of local artisans? Think of ways to generate income from your knowledge, passion, and expertise. Yes, there may be a learning curve, but eventually, you're going to love the extra money flowing in.

HACK

#96

Ask for a Promotion

Being praised for good work is something that makes almost everyone happy, and what better praise can there be for a job well done than a promotion? You know why you should be promoted, but perhaps the timing involved in seeking the promotion could determine whether or not you get it. Is there a major project that needs to be pushed through before it would be wise to ask about getting a promotion? Does someone have to leave before you can move up and into his or her position? Decide when would be the best time to seek a promotion, then mark the date on your calendar and look at it every day. Know that the date is coming and that you need to prepare. Then, when that day arrives, ask!

HACK #97

Say Happy Birthday

Sometimes the smallest things are the most thoughtful and are the things that will truly brighten someone else's day, like wishing people happy birthday. Keep track of your friends' and coworkers' birthdays. It means a lot to people when someone remembers their special day—you'll be surprised how happy hearing "Happy birthday!" makes them. The point isn't really to give people a card or a cake, but rather that you took the time to keep track of their special day and then helped celebrate it with them. Spreading some celebratory happiness on birthdays does wonders for others' morale...and you'll find that sharing the birthday cheer makes you happy too.

Mentor a Child

If you enjoy the company of young people and have the time to mentor a child, consider contacting Big Brothers Big Sisters of America. It is the oldest mentoring organization in the United States, has facilities all over the country, and has been serving youth ages six through eighteen for more than a century. National research statistics published by the organization show the positive and enduring impact adult volunteers ("Bigs") have upon the lives of children ("Littles") they mentor. For example, many of the children involved in the program have better family relations, are more confident about doing schoolwork, are less likely to skip school, and are less likely to use drugs and alcohol. The time you spend mentoring a child could optimize a young person's chances for academic success and be a source of happiness for you and everyone involved in that child's life.

Plan Your Dream Vacation

The anticipation of an event can often bring just as much happiness as the actual event, so start planning the vacation of your dreams now! Even if you don't currently have the funds to take the trip, start looking into the details. You'll notice your spirits start to lift. Maybe you've always wanted to go trekking in the Himalayas or visit a rain forest. No matter your ideal destination, start researching the various aspects of your trip and formulate a plan on how to make your dream a reality.

HACK #100

Party for Independence

Nothing says Fourth of July like a barbecue, so why not plan a party? Get your neighbors to come out of their apartments and houses and socialize by planning an Independence Day street party. If you plan far enough ahead, you can ask your local police department to allow you and your neighbors to rope off your street that day. Hold a Fourth of July cake bake-off, or plan games for different age groups at opposite ends of the street and use the middle for barbecue pits and lawn furniture. It will be a memorable Fourth! Plan on taking lots of pictures that will trigger happy memories years from now.

Raise Money

Nothing makes you feel better about yourself than working to help a noble cause. Help your church, school, or community meet its fiscal responsibilities through fundraising efforts. Successful fundraising depends—at least in part—on showing need and having a donor recognition program that reinforces a sense of belonging. School fundraising events work best when the "fun" in fundraising is emphasized. Some ideas for school fundraisers are having seasonal events, food or juice booths, candy product sales, car washes, and card sales (for prepaid phone cards, pizza cards, or cards for local gift shops). Church fundraising ideas include holding bake sales, holiday boutiques, bingo, and raffles. Raise some money for your school or church and spread the idea that helping others can create happiness for everyone involved.

Don't Burn Bridges

The old adage about not burning your bridges in case you have to cross them again one day very much applies to your career: it's not in your best interest to damage or sever professional relationships. You never know when you might meet those individuals again and have to conduct business together. If you are at least on good speaking terms and have shown respect toward the other party, it will be a lot easier to reestablish a smooth working relationship. Stay optimistic and do your best to safeguard your professional relationships—that way, you can feel happier and more assured that you are doing something vital to keeping your career or job on track.

HACK #103

Play Sports

Get active! You'll feel better. If you prefer team sports to solo sports, join a softball or bowling team or organize a team that includes people from your circle of friends or your business colleagues. Softball teams and bowling leagues play against other teams, so even as you are having fun with friends on your team, you are also potentially making new friends with players from other teams. Psychologists say that people who live isolated lives or lack strong social networks are not as happy as those who form strong bonds and social connections with others and have ongoing support from friends and family.

HACK #104

Invent Something

Do your creative juices start to flow when you see something new? Do you immediately have an idea for making it even more functional or efficient? Do you enjoy figuring out how things work or coming up with innovative ways of doing things? You may have that creative spark that all inventors share. Just tinkering around with your product idea, sketching out drawings, making notes, or even giving your product an original name can bring you happiness. Improve upon an existing product or develop a totally new one. Find a niche in the marketplace: a product that is needed but doesn't yet exist. Who knows? You might have the idea for the next big innovation everyone will be clamoring for.

HACK #105

Go to a Farmers' Market

If there's a farmers' market in your neighborhood, gather your canvas bags or heavy-duty utility bags and head out for a brisk walk to do your grocery shopping. Since you'll be carrying the bags of groceries back home afterward, you'll want to be sure you can carry what you purchase—in other words, buy only what you need and what will fit into your bags. Walking while carrying groceries means you'll be burning a lot more calories than you would be if you drove your car to the store, plus walking is better for the environment. Besides, you'll be getting locally grown produce that is fresher and healthier for you compared to what you can find in a traditional grocery store. Now, that's something to feel good about!

HACK #106

Delegate!

When a job or project is too big for your one brain and your one set of hands, it's time to delegate. If you're not a manager and delegating isn't typically your job, speak to your manager about it. The dictionary says that "delegate" means "to entrust or hand over to another." When your workload is lighter, you can focus more intently on every aspect of your job, meaning that you'll most likely do your job better than you did when you were overloaded. Think of three tasks you could easily hand off to someone else (who is equally qualified for the job) and let that person get to work. Trust your delegates and give them time to do their best work. Everyone will benefit.

HACK
#107

Find a Friend at Work

If there is someone in the company or at your job site whom you trust and who shares your level of integrity and ethics, aligning with them could benefit your professional goals, especially if that person is a supervisor or further along the career ladder than you are. Having someone as a workplace ally means you don't have to feel alone as you navigate through office politics, solve problems, and deal with difficult coworkers. A workplace ally can serve as your sounding board for new ideas, cheer you on when your day is filled with special challenges, and give you pep talks to lift you up when you need a boost.

HACK
#108

Listen to Audiobooks

How can an audiobook make you happy? Because of what it stops you from doing. Think about what you typically do during your commute. Do you talk on your cell? Think about your troubles? Curse the long line of cars ahead of you or at the guy who just cut you off? Instead of doing any of that, do something productive when you are forced to sit in traffic: listen to audiobooks. Buy some books about your area of business or your interests—maybe there's an industry topic you want to know more about, or maybe there's a new language you'd like to learn. You have to be on the road twice a day, so rather than wasting all that time, use it in ways that can return dividends for your future. You may even find yourself looking forward to your commute!

Hit the Sauna

Time spent in a sauna or steam bath is healthy. Why? Sweating releases unwanted materials from the body and improves circulation. Indulging in a sauna or steam bath can eliminate toxins and excess sodium, soothe tense and sore muscles, and enable you to relax into your happy place. Before stepping into a sauna or steam room, though, make sure you're in good health by checking with your doctor. Also, it's important to drink lots of water to replace what you lose from perspiration.

Make a Family Recipe

Strengthen your family connections and forge a stronger family identity by reaching out to your relatives. Host a reunion or small gathering and make a special recipe handed down from previous generations. Then, before your celebration is over, make sure each family member gets a copy of that treasured recipe. Encourage them to pass it along to other relatives too. Your effort creates a tangible link to the past, encourages a celebration of your shared identity, recalls memories, and strengthens family bonds. The beloved relatives who originally made that dish—perhaps even centuries earlier—may have long since passed on, but you can remember them whenever you make your family recipe.

HACK

#111

Bus It

If you only have a couple of days in a city or town, go on a bus tour and let a professional guide show you the sights and tell you about what you're seeing. That kind of informed introduction to an area can help you decide which sites you would like to see more of as well as which areas don't interest you—then you won't waste your precious vacation time wandering around looking for interesting things when you could go straight to them and enjoy yourself.

HACK
#112

Attract the People You Want in Your Life

If you are seeking loyalty and trust in your friendships or in a romantic relationship, first cultivate those qualities within yourself and then demonstrate them to others—in doing so, you become a magnet for exactly what you want. Similarly, if you seek a gentle, loving person as a life partner, avoid someone with a mercurial, volatile, or temperamental nature. Although opposites do sometimes attract, you'll most likely be happiest with a kindred spirit.

HACK
#113

Clear Your Desk Every Day

Time management experts say that a clean desk is important for several reasons. You work more efficiently when you know where your documents and tools are at all times, for example, rather than if you have to search through piles of disorganized material to find them. A clean desk signals to clients and others that you're probably an organized person with efficient and effective work habits. That inspires confidence! So get yourself whatever tidying supplies you need: garbage bags, filing boxes, manila and hanging folders, labels, organizers…and then get to work and join the ranks of happily organized workers.

Volunteer at an Animal Shelter

Helping creatures than cannot help themselves can give your life purpose. Animal shelters around the country are in need of volunteers to help care for and maintain the animals they house in their facilities. Even if you cannot volunteer your time, you can make a monetary donation or contribute items on a local shelter's wish list. Many shelters need easy-to-find things such as peanut butter, plastic bags, bath towels, pet carriers (all sizes for all kinds of pets), and good-quality canned dog and cat food. See a need and fill it. The resulting good feelings are yours to keep.

Play in the Water

There's nothing like playing in the water on a hot summer day. Whether you swim, snorkel, water-ski, deep-sea dive, surf, or head out in a kayak or canoe, there is so much fun to be had in the water! Go buy yourself a bathing suit and join your family or friends for some water play. Of course, be safe: use adequate sunscreen to protect yourself from the sun's harmful rays, wear a hat with a wide brim to shade your face and neck, and avoid the hottest times of the day (when the sun is directly overhead). Also, drink plenty of water to replenish what you sweat away with all that exercise. Now go and have a blast!

HACK #116

Nosh with a Neighbor

Back in the olden days when people didn't have computers, they made friends the old-fashioned way: face-to-face. People would make a casserole or their favorite comfort food and then bring it over to a neighbor and introduce themselves. Why not carry on that tradition? Bring some food over to a new neighbor to welcome them to the building or neighborhood. It doesn't have to be fancy—a cherry pie, a chocolate cake, a loaf of banana bread, and the classic casserole are all easy to make, and they're all delicious. Not really the cooking type? You can bring your neighbor coffee and doughnuts from your favorite coffee shop to give them a warm welcome. You might strike up a new friendship! At the very least, you'll be on good terms with the people you see every day.

HACK
#117

Make Happiness Cards

Create handmade cards for birthdays, anniversaries, engagements, christenings, and other occasions too. You can find blank cards and envelopes at craft stores, and then you can use calligraphy and watercolors or tempera paint to create fun, individualized images. Or design your card on a computer and print it on card stock. Your unique cards will carry messages of caring, thoughtfulness, and, of course, your wishes for abundant happiness.

HACK
#118

Wear Something Sexy

For some parties, the guest list should be kept really short...say, just two people. Your significant other's birthday could be one of those occasions when you show your partner a totally different side of your personality. You don't have to look like a lingerie model, but it might be fun for both of you if you slipped into something sexier than what you normally wear. You could cook a gourmet meal, set the table for two, and then get dressed to meet your partner when he or she comes home from work. You'll both rediscover how exciting a birthday party can be!

Have a Weekly Card Game

Happiness experts have established that a strong support network is vital to having higher life satisfaction levels. Humans are made to love others! Our relationships with our spouses, families, and friends provide us with meaning and happiness. Having a group of friends to do things with on a regular basis is a certain path to happiness, so bust out your cards, invite some friends over, and play your favorite card games. You don't have to play for money—just hanging out with some good friends over food, drinks, and cards (and enjoying a little friendly competition) is all you need.

HACK
#120

Speak Kindly

With a little effort, you can retrain your impulse to blurt out commonly used negative words and phrases in your speech in favor of using positive words that are carefully chosen and thoughtfully offered. For example, phrases like "There's always room for improvement" and "I've seen better from you" are not helpful. In fact, those phrases suggest that someone's actions or thoughts have come up short and don't meet your expectations. You don't want people to say those things to you, so stop saying that to others—instead, offer positive, helpful feedback and comments. Speak honestly but caringly. You'll inspire greatness from others and also generate happiness for yourself too.

Exercise in the Park

If you like stretching, walking, or running, do it in nature—for example, consider joining a group of people who congregate in a nearby park to practice tai chi, qigong, or yoga. Doctors say the best kind of exercise is the kind that you enjoy enough to keep doing consistently. If you like to socialize while working out, meet some friends at a high school football field, on a jogging trail, or at a local park. Breathe some fresh air, take in the lovely sights and sounds of nature, and work out while enjoying the camaraderie of others.

HACK
#122

Do a Fast (No, Really—Don't Eat)

As you fast, your body uses its energy to cleanse itself. Many people believe that fasting can make you more energetic, enable you to think more clearly, and increase your sense of well-being and happiness. There are many types of fasts, from total abstinence of food to eating only certain types of foods or juices. A fast can last for a few hours or for a day or more. People who fast usually drink water or juice to keep their bodies properly hydrated. Because so many debilitating diseases are related to food over-consumption and diets that are high in processed foods, sugar, and other less-than-nutritious ingredients, consider undertaking a fast to detoxify and rejuvenate yourself. Before starting, however, check with your physician to make sure a fast would be a good idea for you.

HACK #123

Avoid Toxins

Happiness is closely linked to good health, and one way to stay healthy is to avoid exposure to various toxic agents. Read and follow safe-use labels on all products containing toxins or carcinogenic agents, including those for your garden or lawn. Instead of spraying chemicals, you might choose pest-resistant plants, pull off pest-infected leaves (and carefully dispose of them), yank out invasive weeds before they re-seed themselves over the yard, and use compost and mulch to create healthy soil. You can also use less toxic products such as soaps and herbicidal oils to treat troublesome garden and lawn pests.

Join the Sierra Club

In today's world where the environment is taking a beating, one way to make your life more meaningful is to join others in working to save the planet. Sometimes things can be accomplished only when working in concert with other like-minded individuals in groups like the Sierra Club or the Rainforest Action Network. Joining a group of people who share your feelings about a common cause can inspire you to do things you might never do on your own. Plus, there is truth to the saying that there's strength in numbers—although one person working alone may not be able to save a rain forest, thousands or millions of people rallying around a single goal might just accomplish it.

HACK

#125

Play Tennis

Playing a game of tennis is a great way to get a workout! Just be sure to warm up your muscles first, and while playing, use proper hitting and serving techniques to prevent injuries. Whether the players are eight years old or they're seniors in their seventies or eighties, almost anyone can play tennis. Learn how to play now and enjoy it for a lifetime. Plus, tennis is social—it's one of those games where you need another player; if you are playing doubles, you'll need three other players. Tennis is a good way to meet new people, get a workout, and feel great at the same time.

HACK #126

Pray

Prayer can center you when things are going right in your life, provide solace and a lift when you feel down, and constantly remind you that you aren't alone. Praying can help you move forward when you feel stuck or provide hope when you need healing. Harold Koenig, MD, associate professor of psychiatry and medicine at Duke University School of Medicine in Durham, North Carolina, has observed that religious people tend to have healthier lives. (And better health means you are more likely to be more satisfied with your life.) Recite a prayer that gives you comfort. Or, if you prefer, you can make up your own prayer. A simple "Thank you!" is a powerful prayer of gratitude. "I need your help" or "Please guide me" are also excellent ways to begin a prayer.

HACK
#127

Snuggle with Something

If you are like many people, as a child you had a little pillow or a security blanket that got you through the night. As an adult facing a crisis, you may wish you had something tangible like that to give you comfort. If you don't have a favorite blanket or pillow, look in the linen closet and see if there's a comfy throw, a worn afghan, or a silky coverlet you could use. Or go to the clearance table at your local department store and pick out something that could become a new favorite security blanket. As a child, you loved your blankey because it was yours and only yours. It had your scent on it. You knew what it felt like and looked like even with your eyes closed. The next time life is not going your way, seek comfort in what's familiar and what makes you feel safe—wrap yourself in your blanket and let your inner child feel safe and comforted.

HACK

#128

Toast the Happy Couple

Remember: the Buddha said that happiness is achieved when your words and your work benefit others as well as yourself. Create an imaginative and highly personalized toast for some newlyweds in your life. Whether you've been asked to offer a toast, provide material for a groom's roast, or write a small wedding speech, make sure the main thread running throughout is a message containing your best wishes for their lifetime of happiness.

Get a Study Buddy

For those times when you want someone to quiz you or share notes from that last lecture, nothing beats having a classmate who's willing to study with you. If there is someone in your class or workshop you find intriguing or who is new to the school or program, ask that person to study with you. Say something to spark a conversation. Imagine being in a new environment and not knowing anyone...and then how welcoming it would feel to have a stranger invite you to study with them. Most likely, the person you ask to be your study buddy will be as supportive of you as you are of them. You both want to excel! It's a win-win for both of you.

Do Crafts with Kids

Get out the box of craft supplies and create something fun, whimsical, or beautiful with some kids in your life. Quality time with children is never time wasted—kids need time with family members to feel loved and wanted. Instead of allowing them to sit in front of the television and be bombarded with (possibly undesirable) messages, establish an hour of family fellowship and watch them thrive. Spending time with kids will make you feel pretty good, too, plus you might end up with some personalized and creative art to keep for yourself.

Give a Farewell Gift

A thoughtful way to send off a friend or neighbor who is moving away is to give that person a gift that will always remind him of the times you shared. If the person who's leaving loves gardening, you could put seeds from your favorite plants into white paper envelopes, then tuck the envelopes into a card to give your friend on his moving day. Or if you used to cook dinner with your neighbor, you could write down some of your favorite recipes for her. That way, when your friend is in her new place, she can plant the flowers or make the dish and think of you.

Have Hope

If something isn't going well in your life—a parent becomes ill, a car hits yours in the parking lot, you overdraw your bank account, the Uber you took to the most important meeting of your life gets snarled in traffic—have hope that circumstances will shift and the situation will improve or resolve. Rather than allowing stress and anxiety to fill you with worry, try to feel hopeful and find the courage to work toward changing what isn't going well. Having a more positive mindset will be better for you emotionally and physically.

Do Puzzles

Keep your brain happy by stimulating it with memory exercises and problem-solving games. Doing daily crossword or number puzzles means your brain gets a sustained cognitive workout every day. Besides, the act of using those little gray cells often brings pleasure as well as mental stimulation!

HACK
#134

Sniff Some Lavender

Whenever you have a bad day, feel exasperated, or struggle to get out of a foul mood, sniff some lavender to restore your serenity. It's easy to see why lavender is one of the most popular scents in aromatherapy. (Scents like citrus, rose, and sandalwood are also pleasant. When you smell them, they can trigger particular memories or experiences because your olfactory nerve carries their scent straight to your brain.) There are many ways to enjoy lavender: use freshly crushed flowers set out in a bowl, set some reeds in a diffuser pot with a splash of lavender essential oil, light some lavender-scented candles, simmer lavender potpourri, or put out sachets of dried lavender. Allow the scent to lift your mood and remember that you never again have to relive a bad day.

Have a Glass of Wine

Unwind with a glass of your favorite wine at the end of an exhausting day. According to a number of studies, wine is good for you if you drink it in moderation and as part of a healthy diet. Wine has phytochemicals (flavonoids and resveratrol) that prevent free-radical molecules from damaging your body's cells. Researchers have shown that drinking dry wine reduces the risk of getting certain cancers as well as heart disease; it also slows the progression of Alzheimer's and Parkinson's diseases. For women, one five-ounce glass per day is good, while men should drink no more than two five-ounce glasses—more than that, and wine does not offer health benefits.

Play with Clay

Maybe you were like a lot of other people and made mud pies as a child. Rediscover what children know about the warm, fuzzy feelings you get from burying your hands in mud—produce a piece of pottery! Spend some happy hours in a pottery class pinching off a ball of clay, centering it on a potter's wheel, shaping it, firing out the impurities, glazing it, and then firing it again to affix the glaze. A pottery class can provide access to clay, a potter's wheel, a kiln, and, of course, an instructor. Alternatively, you can purchase the type of clay that can be fired in your own oven (at lower temperatures than a kiln) and make some beads to string into necklaces.

HACK #137

Get a Massage

A massage is a great way to release the stress and tension you hold in your body. There's nothing comparable to human touch coupled with aromatherapy to transport you into a place of relaxation and peace. Massages are *de rigueur* at day spas. They are also offered at deeply discounted rates at local colleges that run massage therapy training programs. Of course, you could ask your significant other to give you a massage…but that could lead to other activities. Then again, that kind of massage could also relieve stress and put a smile on your face!

Bake Something

You know your way around the kitchen, and you've experimented with a recipe or two to amp up the flavor of your favorite brownies. Why not organize (or participate in) a local bake sale or head off to a county fair with your special culinary creation? Get some validation for your incredible baking skills! There are plenty of online challenges too. Wouldn't it be great to be able to say your pie/cake/trifle/cheesecake was judged the best in the entire competition? Sure, it would—that blue ribbon would give you bragging rights for years to come. Even if you don't win, the simple act of baking is sure to put a smile on your face and some deliciousness in your belly.

HACK #139

Remember That Happiness Is a Journey

If you look back over the past week and remember moments of happiness (even if they're only fleeting) but find that your memories are dominated by moments of stress, anxiety, frustration, exasperation, sadness, resentment, jealousy, impatience, worry, concern, or anger, grab a cup of your favorite tea, put your feet up, and consider this: happy isn't something you feel only *after* you've accomplished everything you want to achieve in life. Nope. It's available to you during every step of the journey...but you make the choice of whether or not you experience that happiness.

Hit the Casino

If you enjoy the occasional visit to a casino for a little gambling and a show, double your pleasure and take a friend along on your next trip. You'll have a pal to share your elation at winning or to commiserate with you if you lose. Besides, there are all those wonderful buffets, and who wants to eat alone? Momentary pleasures are a lot more abundant when you are enjoying a good meal or gambling. (Of course, winning also contributes to pleasure and happiness!) You can feel happy just thinking of all the things you could do if you won a big jackpot, so if you have a few bucks to spare and some free time, call a friend and head to the casino.

HACK #141

Plant an Herb Garden

Gardening gives you the opportunity to work out in the fresh air, and besides, nothing beats fresh-picked herbs when you want to intensify the flavors of salsas, sauces, savory dishes, and drinks (mojitos, anyone?). Tackling weeds and digging holes for plants can also give you a workout. If you love to cook and also appreciate having fresh herbs and produce packed with vitamins, minerals, and other nutrients, consider planting a garden...and then combine the gardening with cooking for a healthier you!

HACK
#142

Give Up Your Seat

Say you're sitting in your seat on a crowded bus or train and you notice an elderly person or a pregnant woman standing, or a small child standing and holding onto his parent's leg. Don't just sit there—get up and offer your seat to the person in need! Think of the good karma you'll be generating. Seniors may not be stable on their feet, young kids can't always reach rails and straps to steady themselves, and pregnant woman are often tired due to, you know, growing another human being. Give up your seat and give these people the safety of sitting. You'll feel good knowing that you showed an act of kindness to another—and you are a better person for having done it.

Create a Vision Board

A sheet of poster paper or a foam board can host images, inspirational words, goals, and dates for accomplishing your goals as well as ideas of new directions to take your dreams. Maybe you want to find a way to help your school establish a theatrical group or an arts program. Perhaps you are an artist yourself and can help make masks, costumes, stage sets, etc. Cut out pictures of representative images from magazines and paste them on your vision board. Do you know other artists who could help you launch such a program? Write their names on your board and contact them. You'll soon learn that a dream doesn't have to be a solo dream—it can come about through a team working together on a shared vision.

HACK #144

Find Pleasure on Bad Days

In spite of any negative circumstances you may be dealing with, find little moments throughout the day to notice the things that give you pleasure. Take time to appreciate seeing the neighbor's yellow roses that have just burst into bloom, the taste of a perfectly ripe and sweet apple, the sound of your favorite music, the painting you bought on your vacation that's now hanging in your room, the feel of your favorite shoes, the warmth of your partner's hand on yours. Savor the gifts of sight, sense, taste, touch, and smell—they're still reacting to your surroundings even as you deal with your lousy day. Take comfort in simply noticing the blessings in the small things and in your short moments of happiness throughout the day.

Be Happier at Work

Think of three things you could do to make yourself happier on the job. Would listening to your favorite music lift your spirits? Would seeing pictures of your family members taped to the bottom of your computer screen inspire you to be happy? Would checking your email at noon instead of when you first arrive at work keep your mood elevated throughout the morning? Find ways to be happy while at work, and your creativity and productivity are likely to rise along with your mood.

Make a Scrapbook

Are you the keeper of family photos? Why not create a scrapbook to trace your family's lineage and to document births, deaths, marriages, and other important events? During this process, you can explore your ancestry or discover your vital health history too. A scrapbook can contain pages with old letters, documents, deeds, and other keepsake documents. You'll not only have hours of fun working on your book and sharing it with relatives during celebrations and holidays, you'll feel a sense of pride and joy from knowing the details of your family's lineage.

Pass Out Fortune Cookies

Host a dinner party for family, relatives, friends, business associates, or members of your community. Serve Chinese food; then, before passing out the fortune cookies, make sure you have inserted little slips of paper containing a compliment or a happiness quote into each cookie. You want to make everyone feel uplifted, happy, and full of good cheer! You can accomplish that by filling their tummies with great food and their minds with pearls of joy.

HACK
#148

Make Some "Me Time"

Plan a little time off just to do some inner reflection. The amount of time is not as important as getting the respite you need. Make your time away a priority! It's a chance for you to clear your head, gather your energy, and get perspective. Retreat to someplace peaceful where you can relax and have a break from the responsibilities of work and family. Don't know of any great retreat places? Take your favorite book and head to a beach. Find a shady bank along the edge of a lake, creek, river, or a pond—someplace where earth and water meet. Sink into your beach chair, tune into the sounds of nature, open your book, and lose yourself in a story. Or just sit back, close your eyes, and let your mind wander. You don't have to do anything while on your retreat—just make space for tranquility and joy to fill you.

HACK #149

Build a Tree House

If you've got a tree in your yard strong enough to support a tree house, get the children in your family involved in helping you create a design for a treehouse, shop for the wood and nails (and all the other construction materials you'll need), and build it. Not only will the children love you for building something that will surely give them many hours of fun memories, but you'll be creating a special space where you can share your inner child with the children in your life!

HACK #150

Text Some Happiness

When you find a happiness quote you love, add it to your email signature so that it will be read by everyone you correspond with throughout your day. Also, when you happen upon a funny meme, hilarious story, joke, or quote, text them to someone you know who needs a boost. If the recipient is having a bad day, your dose of optimism, humor, and happiness may be just what that person needs to start giggling and get back into a joyful groove.

HACK #151

Stop Negative Thoughts

Some of us can get so good at negative or obsessive thinking that we do it without even being consciously aware that we're doing it. You may think *I know I'll make a poor impression at this job interview!* the second you set up the interview. This type of negative thinking can happen faster than you can manufacture happy thoughts to counter them. The good news is that you can learn to interrupt these negative thoughts and then deal more realistically with them. One tactic is to interrupt negative thoughts by simply saying "Stop!" to yourself. Then switch to a positive thought before any other troubling thoughts emerge. A new, more optimistic thought—such as *I will be relaxed, positive, and learn a lot from my interview!*—will allow you to stop your negative thinking. This is a simple but highly effective technique.

Do Something Fun

This may seem simplistic, but many, many people go through their days without *doing* anything fun. Studies have clearly shown that doing something breaks obsessive thoughts. Doing something fun will get you off the beaten track so that you can put things into perspective and get rid of negative feelings or thoughts that have been weighing you down. Not to mention the obvious: it's fun! So whether your fun is skydiving, reading a great novel, swimming, playing with kids, or having a little romantic encounter with your significant other, the lesson here is to stop wishing or thinking about it—get out there and *do* it.

Buy Flowers

Researchers at Harvard University have found that keeping fresh flowers in your living or working space helps keep anxiety and negative moods at bay. People in the study who were around fresh flowers were also more compassionate toward others and more enthusiastic at work, plus they felt a boost of energy. So don't wait for a birthday or Valentine's Day to buy some flowers for yourself or your sweetie! Buy some today.

Go Outside

Sunlight has been proven to help battle depression and negative thoughts and help people feel better. The human body produces vitamin D when exposed to the sun's rays, and when we have vitamin D deficiency, we tend to feel tired, anxious, and depressed. So step into the sunshine for ten to twenty minutes for a boost of happiness! If you can't get outside, try using a light therapy lamp to simulate the same feelings.

Sniff Citrus

The scent of oranges, lemons, grapefruits, and other citrus fruits eases stress and creates positive chemical reactions in your brain. In addition to enjoying the scent of fresh fruit, you can also apply a few drops of diluted citrus essential oil to your pressure points or use diluted citrus oil in a soothing bath. You can also have a nice glass of freshly squeezed orange juice and get the added benefits of drinking vitamin C.

HACK
#156

Put Down Your Phone

Researchers at Kent State University conducted a study of five hundred students and found that frequent smartphone use was associated with lower grades, higher anxiety, and reduced happiness. People who spend a lot of time on their devices are more vulnerable to social comparisons, and that leaves them feeling a sense of emptiness. The fear of "missing out" and feeling inadequate makes it difficult for people to stay present and happy in their own lives. So, a caution: use your smartphone in moderation.

Spend Money on Others

Spending money on other people can boost happiness more than spending money on yourself. According to a Harvard University study, people who bought things for others felt significantly happier immediately after the purchase and upon recollection of the purchase than people who used the money to buy something for themselves. And the good feelings you get from spending on others often leads to doing the same thing in the future. See? Philanthropy grows happiness!

HACK
#158

Try New Positions

Sex is a surefire way to get happy any day of the week, but if you really want to kick up the happiness factor, try some new sexual positions. After all, having sex the same way every time can make even sex boring! Experiment imaginatively before, during, and after sex. You can get in plenty of stretches and a decent cardio workout as well, not to mention get all of those pleasurable endorphins flowing. If you can't dream up any new ways to turn on, tantalize, or titillate your partner, try reading the *Kama Sutra* or visit your local bookstore or Amazon.com for books that can provide some insight. Bring the heat back into your relationship with some imaginative sex.

Exercise

Exercise releases endorphins throughout your body, creating feelings of happiness. While many people find it hard to motivate themselves to exercise, the mood boost you get after exercising is worth the effort. Researchers from Penn State found in a recent study that people who were more physically active had more pleasant-activated feelings than people who did not exercise. Additionally, exercise energizes you, helps you feel less stressed out, boosts your confidence, and can even fight insomnia. Any physical activity that gets you to break a sweat helps you build happiness—even a brisk walk works! So get that blood pumping and get happy.

Eat Turmeric

From golden milk to spiced rice, turmeric has made big news headlines for its anti-inflammatory properties. But the active compound in turmeric—curcumin—also has antidepressant qualities. It can cause an increase in serotonin and dopamine (the "feel-good" chemicals) in your brain and help boost your mood. And it's not just straight turmeric that gives you this mood boost but also dishes that contain the spice, like curries.

Host a Dinner Party

Hosting a party can be stressful, but it can also be a whole lot of fun, especially when the only thing on the agenda is good food. Sharing food is about more than just eating and drinking—you're sharing meaningful and pleasurable moments with great friends. If everyone has fun, make it into a regular thing, rotating the location to each member's home. Planning and preparing a gourmet meal is not necessarily as difficult as you might think. All you really need is an idea of what to make, some fresh, wholesome ingredients, and a few basic pantry staples.

Hit the Snooze Button

Some mornings, there is no greater pleasure than being able to hit the snooze button and go back to sleep for ten more luxurious minutes. Set your alarm clock for ten minutes earlier than you really have to get out of bed; then, when the alarm goes off, you'll have the joy of knowing you can go back to sleep and ignore it. Sometimes that small triumph over the alarm clock can make the rest of your morning seem better.

HACK #163

Assume the Best in Others

Happy, optimistic people give others the benefit of the doubt and expect to like other people (unless given a reason not to). Try adopting that mindset: when you meet someone new, choose to see that person as a potential friend whose company you might enjoy. Try this idea with your existing relationships too! Don't assume a friend you haven't seen in a while doesn't care about you—instead, give that person the benefit of the doubt and assume that your friend's absence has nothing to do with you.

Live Close to Work

Commuting is a stress-inducing, anxiety-filled activity that can wear down even the most patient of people. In a study of over one thousand employed Americans, the times of the day when they felt the worst was during their commute to and from work. In fact, people felt happier while *at* work and even while doing housework at home than they did when commuting. Couples with one partner commuting more than forty-five minutes have a 40 percent higher divorce rate. If you have a choice about where you live with respect to your job location, do yourself a favor and make your commute a reasonable distance.

Reminisce

The happiness that can come from reminiscing about happy memories is as real as the feelings that happened during the actual event. In fact, people who frequently reminisce about positive life events are the most likely to be happy. So take photos, make scrapbooks, bring home souvenirs, call an old friend, watch your favorite movies…do whatever you need to do to relive those positive memories.

HACK #166

Buy Small Things

Instead of buying the latest smartphone, the coolest new car, or the best new laptop, buy several small things: fancy chocolates, a few nice candles, some music for your phone. It will actually make you happier to indulge in frequent small pleasures than to buy more extravagant (and expensive) delights. After all, you don't get twice as much happiness from buying a car that is twice as expensive as another model! Use some of that money to pay for a weekend away with your partner. You'll get far more satisfaction from your getaway weekend than you would from the luxury car.

HACK #167

Sit Up Straight

Everyone knows that sitting up straight and not slouching is good for your body. In fact, poor posture causes extra wear and tear on joints and ligaments, increases the likelihood of accidents, makes your lungs less efficient, and can lead to tension headaches and back pain. However, more and more people are losing their proper posture due to their devices. The condition known as "tech neck," derived from staring down at a computer screen or phone, is becoming a real problem. In addition, slouching doesn't just make you look bad, it can make your body feel bad too. When you slouch in a chair, your brain actually thinks you are tired or unsure of yourself. Whereas sitting straight can boost your confidence, give you more energy, and make you more productive. So sit up straight! You'll feel better, look better, and have more confidence.

Stop Complaining

Seeing as the brain has a tendency to focus on the negative, complaining may in fact be a natural human reaction. Still, that doesn't mean complaining is the best reaction. Dwelling on how much something sucks is not good for your body or your mood. Besides, when has complaining ever gotten you anywhere? All it does is reinforce negativity. So rather than complaining about something, try to focus on something else, something positive. You'll be happier.

Don't Settle

It's tough to leave your comfort zone, which is why so many of us reach a place of comfort in our jobs or lives and then stop: we stop learning, we stop growing, we stop changing. But stagnation results in less happiness! Of course, just changing for the sake of change won't lead to happiness, either. Getting a new job will be exciting at first, for example, but as soon as the novelty wears off, you'll be back in your same rut. Instead of letting that happen, try to continue making improvements in your life. Move well past your comfort zone if you have to—don't settle for less.

HACK
#170

Don't Be a Pushover

Being a pushover means that you tend to do things you don't want to because you'd rather avoid confrontation. You don't stand up for your opinions or ideas and you are easily taken advantage of. However, being a pushover doesn't make you weak, it just means you lack the tools of defense. First learn how to express how you feel. If something doesn't feel right to you or bothers you, speak up about it. Next learn how to say no if you feel you don't have the time to do something. Then pick your battles and fight constructively—meaning you should be direct and honest but calm. Remember you shouldn't be passive in your life: communicate your preferences and ask for what you want. You don't have to steamroll over other people to do that, but do be assertive and set boundaries for yourself that you don't want others to break. You'll find that assertiveness increases self-esteem, makes you feel like your needs are being better met, and can improve your relationships.

Drink Coffee

Coffee is the nectar of the gods for many of us, and for good reason—the caffeine in coffee gives us energy, fights off depression, and boosts our mood. A recent study showed that just the *smell* of coffee can make you feel less stressed. In addition, coffee provides you with easily absorbable antioxidants, is good for your liver, can make you feel happier, can fight your risk of getting skin cancer (if you're a woman), can reduce your risk of type 2 diabetes, and can keep your brain healthier for longer than a non-coffee drinker. The caveat with caffeine, though, is that the more you consume, the less you reap its benefits. So to really get happy from your coffee, enjoy it in moderation.

Drink Water

Staying hydrated gives you more energy, improves your skin's texture and color, and gives your body what it needs to function properly. Even mild dehydration can have cognitive effects on your mood, decrease your memory, and impact brain function. In fact, many people mistake symptoms of dehydration for symptoms of depression! If you are feeling lethargic, have difficulty concentrating, or have trouble remembering things, you may need to drink more water. When you get enough water, your body will feel healthier and happier.

Write Down What You Dream of Doing

Are you feeling a little lost and lacking direction in your life? Try sitting down in a quiet place and thinking about what you really want to do. Write it down. Maybe there's a place you've always wanted to visit or a job you've always wanted to try or a food you've always wanted to cook. Your goals can be anything. Look at your list and think about how you can accomplish those things. You know that doing those things will make you happy, so why not finally do them?

Ask "Do You Got a Problem?"

This is an almost immediate happiness technique that comes from several two-bit New York movie gangsters (just kidding, it's from author Eckhart Tolle) that asks you to think if you've got a problem. Here's what you do, simply ask yourself, "Do I have a problem right now at this moment?" When you really think on this matter the answer is usually no. Most problems are things you imagine coming down the road or things that happened in your past. When you think about this present moment and realize you don't have a problem right now, you'll give yourself a little mood boost.

Connect with Old Friends

Having a network of longtime connected friends is a proven stress-buster. If you haven't seen your old friends in a while, it's time to reconnect with them. Sure, you may have grown and changed since you last spent time together, but the new experiences you've all had will give you plenty to talk about. Don't fret about how things used to be—just find new ways to connect with your longtime friends. You've gone through a lot together! Remember the good times and keep your ties strong.

Clean Your Space

Cleanliness may be next to godliness, but it usually isn't high on most people's happiness scale. Decluttering your home, however, will help you declutter your life—when your home is clean and organized, your mind feels organized too. A clean home environment brings less stress and helps you feel calmer and in turn happier. If you are facing a big mess and feeling overwhelmed, try throwing away/donating five items every day.

Wear More Color

Studies have shown that color can enhance your mood and make you feel better about yourself. The takeaway? While black may be slimming for your body, it isn't doing much for your mind. Get out of your black clothing rut and add a little color to your wardrobe! You'll notice an improved sense of confidence, and happiness will follow.

Eat Something Spicy

The hot burn you get when you eat something spicy is not technically a taste but a sensation of pain. Capsaicin, the chemical in spicy food, binds to pain receptors in the body when you eat it, causing your body to interpret the feeling as pain and your brain to release feel-good endorphins to offset your body's reactions. That means you'll get a rush of good feelings when you eat spicy food.

Give an Extra 10 Percent

Everyone gets to a point where it seems like it's time to give up on something, whether it's a project or a relationship. When you reach that point, before you give up, give another 10 percent of your effort. If you were already all in, then ratchet up to 110 percent and try again. Even if the endeavor doesn't work out in the end, you'll know you gave it all you had, and that in and of itself will make you feel happier. Often, we regret something most when we feel like we could have put in a little more effort. Don't let that happen to you!

HACK

#180

Don't Take It Personally

We all do it: when someone is rude to us, we tend to get offended even if we don't even know the person. Instinctively, we think we did something wrong to make that person act like a jerk to us. Usually, though, that's not the case—the other person is really the one with the problem. People tend to take out their pent-up anger and deep-rooted issues on those around them. Try to realize that and stop taking everything so personally. The next time somebody calls you a name or says you aren't good enough, don't take it personally. It's not about you. When you internalize that, you'll let go of the need to be perfect for others, and you'll start to see yourself more clearly (and be more happy).

HACK
#181

Don't Care What Others Think of You

We constantly seek acceptance from those around us and try to find satisfaction from the approval of others, but in the end, we still feel empty. You may dress a certain way or do certain things to fit in with those around you, but all you achieve is changing yourself. The secret to becoming a happier person is to relinquish the need to impress others and to realize that the only person who needs your approval is you. Sure, it's nice to be praised for your work and it's nice to make your parents proud, but those shouldn't be the main reasons you do what you do. Everything you are and everything you achieve should be only for you! Pleasing others is an added bonus.

Stop Thinking You Are Missing Something

People always say "I'll be happier when I lose ten pounds" or "I'll be happier when I get that job" or "I'll be happier when I go on my dream vacation," but none of those statements are true. Happiness comes from living in the moment, not from some future abstract event. If you put your happiness on hold for a future event, you are robbing yourself of having happiness now.

Take Charge of Your Own Happiness

You can select your mood for the day the same way you choose your clothes, so choose to be happy! No one else can make you happy—you are in charge of your own happiness. If you aren't happy with yourself, you won't feel happy. Don't let anyone take your happiness away from you.

Accept What You Cannot Change

There are some things you cannot change: your height, your past, your upbringing. There is no sense in letting these things weigh you down. You need to keep moving forward and learning from the mistakes you've made. Spending your time worrying about things you cannot change will only rob you of happiness. Instead, focus on what you do have and be grateful.

Go Easy on Yourself

All too often, we are our own worst enemies. While it's good to be aware of mistakes you've made in the past and improvements you can make in the future, beating yourself up on a regular basis is a surefire way to wind up singing the blues. In fact, self-criticism can just make you more miserable. So instead of dwelling on your past failures, focus on how and why you value yourself. This shift will make you stronger, more productive, less stressed...and, yes, happier.

Talk to Happy People

When you meet people who are positive thinkers and content with their lives, ask what makes them feel that way. Maybe ask if you can interview them as part of research you're doing for an article about happy people. Pose questions in a way that will draw out their answers—rather than asking simple yes or no questions, ask the kind of questions that will prompt long and thoughtful responses. Encourage them to share their tips for cultivating a happy life. Afterward, if you are feeling ambitious, you really can write that article and pitch it to a local newspaper or neighborhood newsletter.

HACK
#187

Take a Class

Is there something you've always been intrigued about doing but never had the knowledge to attempt? Maybe you've always wanted to create stained-glass art or cook a gourmet meal or create your own jewelry. Whatever it is, enroll in a hands-on class and learn about it. A class can walk you through an in-depth exploration of your interest, provide all the necessary materials needed for a project, and provide you with a knowledgeable instructor who can guide you along the path to success. You'll meet new people in your class too. Who knows? One (or more) of them might become friends, and you might wind up spending many happy hours together creating works of art.

Give a Gift

Another way get some happiness is to perform a small act of kindness and give someone else a gift. Gifts can be anything. For example, you could buy someone's coffee ahead of you in the coffee line. Just tell the cashier "That woman's coffee is on me" and then smile at the person and tell her to have a great day. Or maybe you could pick some flowers from your garden and take them to a neighbor, or offer someone your seat on the bus. You'll be surprised at how good you'll feel after giving someone else a gift.

The gift-giving experience can be a way to find deeper meaning in life. Think of gifts that do not cost any money: a smile for a stranger, holding a door open for someone, or helping someone put groceries in their car. In just a few minutes, you could give a gift for no reason at all that could have a profound impact on someone else's life.

Write Three Things You Love about Yourself

Do you have an inner critic who constantly reminds you that your nose is too big or your hips are too wide or your chest is too flat? Think of three wonderful things you love about yourself and write them on a card. They don't have to be physical attributes—they could include things like "I love my compassionate nature" or "I love my ability to immediately put other people at ease" or "I love the fact that I have great inner strength." Tape the card to your mirror, computer, refrigerator, or any other place where you'll be frequently reminded of the gifts that are uniquely yours.

Start a New Tradition

Remember when you and your friends went on that impromptu road trip that turned into a crazy adventure? Perhaps something wonderful and spontaneous occurred as you were preparing to leave for summer break. Maybe you had a memorable time on the night before Thanksgiving or during the afternoon of the first snowfall of the year. Or maybe you had a pillow fight that ended with everyone making popcorn and s'mores and watching old movies in their pajamas. Whatever may have happened, if the event still evokes powerful memories for everyone involved, make it a tradition! Brainstorm with your friends or family about making a new tradition that you'll be able to reminisce about and reenact in the future. Traditions are all about happy times and bonding, so why not start a new one today?

Binge Watch Your Favorite Show

Experts say that too much TV is not good for you, but who can deny the pleasure of sitting down with some popcorn and a few drinks and watching the full story arc of your favorite show in one night? From the first introductions to the last goodbyes, sit on a comfy couch and envelop yourself in your favorite TV world for a night.

Treat Yourself

Your apartment needs dusting, the dishes are still standing in the sink, the floor needs mopping, and you haven't even gotten around to doing the laundry...but just for today, leave it all alone. Take the time to indulge in something that makes you feel peaceful and relaxed. For example, go to your favorite coffee shop and order your favorite brew. Or sit on your porch and gaze out into your backyard and enjoy the greenness. Go to the beach and just feel the wind on your face, the sun on your back, the calmness of the moment.

HACK
#193

Volunteer with Habitat for Humanity

If doing hands-on, helpful construction work appeals to your social conscience, swing a hammer, carry some lumber, and otherwise help build a home for a poor family. Habitat for Humanity is a nonprofit organization that works in tandem with volunteers in communities worldwide to build houses for low-income people. (Former president Jimmy Carter and his wife spend a week every year swinging hammers to help erect affordable shelters for the poor on behalf of Habitat for Humanity.) If you believe you could be doing more to help the less fortunate, then grab your hammer and work up a sweat working with Habitat for Humanity alongside people like yourself.

HACK #194

Forgive Someone

No doubt you've heard the saying that when you refuse to forgive someone, you are just continuing to let that person hurt you. Why do that to yourself? Try and forgive. Forgiveness leaves your memories intact but removes and even transforms the emotional stings—it's an effective way to diminish painful feelings so that you can create more pleasurable ones. Forgiveness is not an erasure of the past; rather, it's a great way to change the emotional projections that a memory carries (because *you* attached deep meaning to what happened when it occurred). Forgiveness reduces the energy you'd be spending to maintain your anger toward someone who has offended and hurt you. Forgiveness is good for your body and soul.

Give to a Stranger

It's as simple as this: giving feels good. Effort spent identifying what another person can really benefit from in a lasting way stirs feelings of empathy and love. Giving without knowing the other person can be even more rewarding. Giving anonymously—and spontaneously—can feel extremely gratifying. This manner of giving means not expecting something in return, and that's the true meaning of altruism. Giving from your heart connects you with mankind, expands and fulfills that *you* in you (some call that your soul), and boosts serotonin levels.

#196

Play

Playing stimulates your brain's pleasure centers: your basal ganglia (the part that coordinates movement and feeling) and your deep limbic system (home of your emotional intensity and passion). The combined stimulation alerts your prefrontal cortex (the thinking part) to tell you that you're having fun! To maximize your enjoyment and to reinforce these good feelings, your brain starts pumping out that neurotransmitter we love so much: dopamine. The upshot is that your brain goes on a happy holiday. The more pleasurable experiences you create through play, the happier you'll be.

Break a Bad Habit

You can train your brain to abandon negative habits by teaching your brain to associate them with neutral or even bad circumstances (the latter as a punishment). For example, instead of getting yourself worked up over the fact that you smoke one cigarette a day, remove all thought from the act of smoking that one cigarette. Don't attach any negative or positive actions, thoughts, or emotions to it. Neutralize any associations. Once you've taken the pleasure away from smoking, it will be less appealing. If that tactic doesn't work for you, try following up the act of smoking that cigarette with something unpleasant, such as scrubbing your toilet, paying bills, or listening to heavy metal music at a ridiculously high volume. Whatever it is, it should be something that you genuinely *dislike*, and you should force yourself to do it *every* time you have that cigarette (or, if you can't bring yourself to do that, enlist someone else to help with the punishment, such as a close friend). Soon enough, the cigarette will probably not seem worth the hassle, and you will abandon the habit.

Laugh—A Lot

Laughing is the cure for what ails you. Laughing has amazing benefits, including beating back a tide of stress hormones (cortisol, in particular), giving your body a healthy break, lowering your blood pressure, strengthening your immune system, and generating the release of endorphins (those wonderful happiness hormones). Laughter also provides a physical and emotional release, making you feel cleansed afterward. And it's a great internal workout for your body!

Ditch the Sugar

While your body requires a pretty constant supply of glucose (i.e., blood sugar) in order to function properly, constantly eating refined sugars and slurping down sodas is not the best way to maintain healthy glucose levels. On the contrary, researchers at the Salk Institute in California found that high glucose levels resulting from quick, easily digested sugars slowly but surely damages cells everywhere in the body, especially in the brain. In addition to the unneeded extra calories that these sources of refined sugar provide, sugar can also depress your immune system, depress your mood, and lead to feeling fatigued.

HACK
#200

Get Some B$_{12}$, Baby

In a recent study, it was shown that people who were deficient in vitamin B$_{12}$ were twice as likely to suffer from severe depression compared to those without a deficiency. The lack of B$_{12}$ seemed to cause a buildup of serotonin in the brain that led to the neurons having trouble releasing the serotonin as they normally would. To get more B$_{12}$ and to naturally boost your happiness, try eating foods rich in B$_{12}$: eggs, milk, clams, beef, oysters, crab, and tuna. If you're a vegan or vegetarian or are just not a fan of those foods, you could also take a supplemental B$_{12}$ vitamin.

Be Positive

Every thought releases brain chemicals. Being focused on negative thoughts effectively saps the brain of its positive forcefulness and slows it down. Negative thoughts can even dim your brain's ability to function, resulting in depression. On the flip side, focusing on positive, happy, hopeful thoughts produces chemicals that create a sense of well-being. These chemicals help your brain function at peak capacity. There are hundreds of benefits to being positive, among them the fact that being positive—especially around friends and family—will make it easier for others to be positive too. So turn that frown upside down! Give your brain the juice it needs to function at its peak capacity so that you—and your brain—can feel good about life.

Eat Your Greens

Dark leafy greens like spinach, collard greens, and kale are high in folate, which is important because your body can't make folate—you must obtain it through foods or supplements. Folate helps decrease negative thoughts and depressive symptoms by increasing dopamine in the brain. And a bonus: these greens will also help keep your brain sharp well into old age!

Listen to Music and Sing Along

Have you ever noticed how good you feel when you hear certain song or a how an old tune can bring back a flood of happy memories? That's because music is a mood enhancer. Listening to music releases dopamine (our favorite feel-good hormone) into your system and makes you feel happy. In addition, singing a song triggers a tiny organ in your inner ear called the saccules. It's connected to a part of your brain that registers pleasure, making you feel good no matter how good of a singer you are!

Drink Green Tea

Green tea has been shown to reduce stress levels. In fact, a study showed that people who drank five or more cups of green tea a day had 20 percent lower levels of stress than those who only drank one cup of green tea. As an added bonus, green tea also helps with weight loss and helps prevent heart disease, high blood pressure, certain cancers, and osteoporosis. So drink green tea to be happy and healthy!

Quit Nagging

Not only does nagging someone to do something rarely lead to a good outcome (or even work particularly well), nagging also makes the nagger feel angry and mean. You'll get a mood boost when you quit nagging! Try kinder, more persuasive tools to get some help when you need it...or just do the task yourself. Often simply coming out and asking someone (one time!) to do a task is more effective than getting on their case about it. And you'll feel better about yourself too.

Go to Bed Angry (Occasionally)

Studies have shown that unleashing your anger over every inconvenience is not actually helpful. In fact, expressing your anger over minor, fleeting annoyances actually amplifies bad feelings, while not expressing anger often allows it to dissipate. So perhaps try going to bed angry when the situation is not critical—you'll wake up feeling better and happier.

HACK #207

Be Tough

The happiest people are not always the people who win; rather, they are the people who don't give up when they lose. So when things go wrong, be calm and be tough. Keep pushing forward even when it feels like you are alone. Self-pity is not helpful and will not lead to long-term happiness. Believe in yourself, fight for yourself, and stay strong.

HACK #208

Be Busy, but Not Rushed

Rushing or feeling rushed is a one-way street to unhappiness, but feeling busy and productive actually leads to happy feelings. It's true: boredom can be overwhelming and burdensome. Balanced free time is essential, though, so strive to lead a productive life at a comfortable pace. This also means you will have to say no to some things (another happiness hack!).

HACK #209

Stop Blaming

People make mistakes. Vendors don't meet shipping schedules; significant others fail to remember important dates…it happens. But blaming others for problems that arise in your life is fruitless. Besides, perhaps you actually have a share in the blame. Maybe you didn't communicate clearly or maybe you didn't provide enough training. Maybe you just asked too much of someone. Taking responsibility when things go wrong instead of blaming someone else isn't being a pushover! It's actually empowering, because that way, you're able to focus on learning from your mistakes. That's how we all get smarter. And when you're smarter about handling life, you are happier.

Get Rid of Your Ego

Letting your ego be wounded and letting yourself feel offended creates destructive energy. This negative energy often leads us to attack others, which then produces counterattacks. Living in a state of permanent back-and-forth competition is detrimental to yourself and those around you. Your ego loves to judge people—it tries to measure people by their appearance, what kind of possessions they own, or other meaningless standards. It loves to divide people into winners and losers. But these feelings will pull you away from other people and leave you feeling isolated, bitter, and alone. Go beyond the constant clamoring of your ego to be right! Instead, try to enjoy your life and accept others as they are.

Floss

Can flossing make you happy? Yes. It comes down to self-care and self-respect. You know that flossing is important for your oral health and can help prevent a myriad of nasty symptoms, from bad breath to gum decay, but let's be honest—you hardly ever floss, right? If you can't commit to something as simple (but important!) as flossing to improve your health, then you are most likely not making yourself a priority in other areas of your life, either. Commit to your health and yourself with a little flossing, and you'll notice you will start to prioritize yourself more.

Keep a Journal

Keep a journal and commit to writing in it every day. Even if you don't have anything to say, you can just write how you felt about the day or about some things that happened that made you feel happy or grateful. Some days you'll write a lot and some days you'll write very little, but no matter what, commit to writing each day. A journal also serves as a record of the things you have accomplished and the goals you have met, and it helps prove that you have overcome problems in the past. Going back and reading your journal can give you inspiration and motivation, plus it can be cathartic to get your feelings onto paper rather than keeping them bottled up inside.

HACK #213

Read a Book/ Article on a Subject You Know Nothing About

People have a natural desire to learn and progress. Learning something new can help you build self-confidence and self-efficacy. Learning will also fuel your creativity—learning something new in one area can often help you make connections between other seemingly unrelated things. In other words, learning something new about one topic can trigger you to think differently about something that's already going on in your life. You'll also get a sense of satisfaction and a boost in self-esteem for having increased your skills and knowledge.

HACK
#214

Have a Plan for Each Day

You don't need to plan every minute of your day in advance—in fact, that would probably end up causing you a great deal more stress and worry than it would spark happiness—but you should try to get the most out of your workday so that you can relax and enjoy your time away from work. One of the best ways to be effective is to plan your day in intervals. For example, work for an hour, take a ten-minute break, work another hour, take a thirty-minute break, and so on. Because your brain cannot concentrate for longer than a few hours at a time, planning your day in intervals can improve your productivity.

HACK
#215

Don't Work
So Much

Overworking yourself will not bring you happiness. It is not something to be proud of or something to brag about. No one at their end of their life thinks *I wish I had spent more time preparing for that presentation!* In fact, workers who work more than eleven hours a day have a higher risk of depression than those who work a standard seven- or eight-hour day. Want to know what overworking will get you? Sick, stressed, off-balance, disengaged, and less smart. In a study using MRI scans, researchers at Yale found that people who felt stressed out on a regular basis had smaller brain volumes than less stressed-out subjects.

HACK #216

Stop Worrying

We are a society of worriers, but in reality most of the terrible things that we envision happening never do. We are afraid of what might happen (or not happen) with respect to things we can't change (or won't be able to change) and what other people think about us. We worry and we hesitate, and as a consequence, we wind up thinking longer about doing something rather than just *doing* it. Meanwhile, weeks, months, and years pass, and we are still worried and still unhappy. If you want to be happier, put aside fear and worry and do something! Start something; take a first step. The only thing you should worry about is wasting your days and your life and not doing what you dream about doing.

HACK
#217

Don't Be Afraid to Admit You Don't Know

No one wants to look stupid, and you may think it's easier to just nod your head or say that you understand something. But in reality, you will look more foolish if you pretend to understand something than if you don't. When you're in a workplace or faced with an intimidating person or situation, it can be difficult to admit you don't know something. Oftentimes you may be fudging your way through a conversation and come to a point where you don't know the answer to something. You could pretend that you do (and risk getting called out later or thrown into a situation you can't handle) or you could just admit you don't know. Saying you don't know something or didn't understand something will actually give you credibility. You might also get a better explanation of whatever you didn't understand or more time to figure something out.

Play with a Pet

Play with your pets! Take your dog for a walk or play with your cat for a few minutes each day. Feel the unconditional love and joy you can get from an animal. The act of caring and providing for a pet can give you satisfaction too. Pets require constant care and attention, and being able to give your pet that support can make you feel accomplished. Don't have a pet? Stop an owner on the street and ask to pet their dog, or watch pet videos online. A recent study found that just watching cat videos online can boost a person's energy and increase feelings of happiness.

HACK
#219

Compliment Someone

There are many ways that complimenting someone can lead to happiness. In addition to the good feels you'll get by making someone else happier, a genuine compliment helps build trust between people. It also is more likely to lead to someone giving you a compliment in return, which can make you feel special. That's not to say that you should pay someone a compliment just to get one in return, but one good reason to compliment others is that you'll be promoting a happiness chain that can help change attitudes and build a positive rapport among your coworkers and friends.

HACK #220

Be Consistent

Treat everyone you meet the same way: don't treat the president of your company better than her intern. And don't treat your coworkers with kindness and respect and then come home and take your frustrations out on your significant other or family. Being consistent not only makes other people feel better about you—treating people equally makes you appear fair and open-minded—it will help you feel less critical and judgmental.

HACK #221

Be There for the Little Moments

It's important to be there for people you care about during the big moments of life: weddings, births, funerals, first days of school. But aside from that, being there for the little moments is what truly lets people know you care about them. Your friend had a bad day at work? Grab some wine to share and listen to his problems. Your niece is having a problem at school? Take her out for ice cream and help her come up with a solution. It's the seemingly smaller events in life that can truly shape us, so be present for your loved ones in those moments. They won't forget it.

HACK

#222

Stop Checking Social Media So Much

Social media is an amazing service that helps us connect with the world. The problem, though, is that social media can also disconnect you from actual interactions with people. You don't have to quit email/*Twitter*/ *Facebook*/*Instagram*/*Tumblr* cold turkey—just check it a couple of times a day and then be done with it. If people truly need to get in touch with you, they can call you. (You know, that other function of your phone!)

HACK
#223

Shorten the Time You Feel Pissed Off

People will piss you off—it's part of life, and feeling frustrated is a natural reaction that you often can't control. But what you *can* control is how long you let that feeling control you. Don't allow yourself to become stuck in feelings of anger or resentment! That will only take you down a negative path, one that will let the anger in you grow. Instead, feel pissed off, acknowledge the wrong that was done to you, and then start to let it go. Holding anger inside will just poison your happiness.

HACK
#224

Stop Saying "I'm Fine"

"I'm fine." "Things are fine." "We're doing fine." "Fine" is one of the most over-used and meaningless words people say today. You should never answer "fine" when someone asks you how you are doing. Take a few moments to actually *think* about how you are feeling and then give an appropriate answer: "I'm bored." "I'm nervous." "I'm great." Take the time to think about your feelings instead of giving a throwaway response. Who knows? You might even inspire the person who's asking to think more about their feelings as well!

Don't Interrupt

Interrupting someone isn't just rude—it sends the message that you don't care about the other person. When you interrupt what someone is saying, what you're doing is telling that person, "I don't care enough about you to listen to what you are saying so that I can understand you—I am just listening until I can decide what *I* want to say next." Genuinely listen to what the other person is saying. Focus on what the other person is telling you and try to actually understand their point rather than just thinking about your counterpoint. Ask questions about what the other person is saying. Your interlocutor will feel appreciated and valued, and in turn, you'll feel happier that you took the time to listen.

HACK
#226

Get Rid of Some of Your Stuff

You've no doubt heard that things won't bring you happiness…yet we all still buy more and more stuff. Buying things doesn't make us happy for many reasons: possessions are only temporary, possessions require maintenance, possessions make us worry about damage and theft, and no matter how much you have, someone else will always have more. So instead of looking to fill your happiness void with buying more things, try having fewer things. Redirect your buying desires to other pursuits that are more lasting.

Don't Plot Revenge

When someone wrongs you, your first reaction may be to devise a plan to inflict similar pain on that person. You may even feel like doing so will make you feel better about your own pain. In reality, though, seeking revenge does not cancel out your pain—all it does is continue the cycle of pain. There is a famous saying: "Before seeking revenge, first dig two graves." That makes sense, because when you seek revenge, you are hurting yourself in the process. Rise above the situation and move forward. You don't want to let pain suck you into a negative place.

Talk to a Kid

That old saying about wisdom coming from the mouths of babes is more true than you might think. Try to regularly talk to someone under the age of seven. What you will discover is a fierce zest for life, a refreshing outlook, and a no-nonsense attitude about what it takes to be happy. Want to learn what it's like to really enjoy a day? Talk to a kid and understand the simple joys of life.

Talk to a Senior

Want to truly appreciate the world and the wonders of time? Talk to a senior. Talk to people who have literally seen the world change, not just in terms of technology and convenience, but also through the atrocities of war and the moments that changed history. The perspective and knowledge you can gain from seniors and maybe even apply to your own life is monumental.

Don't Dwell

The past is a valuable thing: it holds valuable memories and teaches us lessons. Learn from those lessons and learn from those mistakes…and then let them go. If something bad has happened, see it as an opportunity to learn something you didn't know. If someone else made a mistake, see it as an opportunity to be forgiving and understanding. The past does not define you. Think of the past as practice and training, letting you learn lessons so that you don't repeat them. Don't dwell on the bad aspects of the past and don't live in the pain of old hurts. Move forward!

Start with the Basics

Want to get quickly overwhelmed and give up on making a positive change as soon as you've begun making it? Then try to handle a big change all at once. It won't work. Tackling a big lifestyle change should start with small, basic steps. If you try to do to much too quickly, you will get frustrated, resent the change, and eventually give up on it. Instead, start with small, easy-to-manage steps and gradually add more steps over time.

Be Okay with People Not Liking You

"What other people think of you is none of your business." This quote is true on so many levels—what other people think of you should not affect the way you live your life. Some people will not like you no matter what you do, so it's no use trying to change yourself to meet someone else's expectations. Be yourself, express your thoughts as you see fit, and be comfortable in your own skin. If others don't appreciate you, that is their issue, not yours.

Research Stuff

Learning has been widely documented as a key variable when it comes to health and longevity. When people are engaged in doing and learning new things, their well-being and happiness increase significantly. Find something you have always wanted to know about and set out to research it! Learn how it works, where it came from, what it does, anything and everything you can. Expand your mind, and not just on a superficial level—really explore this new thing with ferocity. Your mind and your mood will thank you.

Don't Preach

Sure, you've probably done some great stuff in your life. Sure, you may have great education or training or experience. But you know what? None of that makes you smarter or better or more insightful than anyone else. It just makes you unique. The more you learn or the higher you rise, the more likely you are to think that you know everything—and the more likely you are to feel like you should tell everyone else what to do. But preaching at someone is really just a form of judging. It's speaking to them as if they have a lower status in life or are less intelligent, and while they may hear you, they certainly won't *listen* to you. Preaching at someone rarely leaves you feeling good about yourself—instead, it robs you of your happiness.

HACK
#235

Have a Sense of Meaning

What do you want to do with your life? If you want to be happier about your work and your future, then find something that has real meaning for you. No matter what your goal is or how big it is, research has proven that if your goal has a sense of meaning for you, you will be happier pursuing it. If you know your work has a meaningful and positive impact on others or the world, you will be happier pursuing that path.

Love Someone

A decades-long study at Harvard University came to the conclusion that the ability to be intimate with another person was one of the strongest predictors of health and happiness. Those people who were commitment-phobic or intimacy-phobic were among the unhappiest people. (Of course these findings only apply to "rational" love and not unrequited, abusive, obsessive, or harmful love.) So, choose a partner whom you can love and respect and who feels the same way about you. Show affection: kiss, cuddle, and compliment your partner often. Share your troubles and your triumphs, your fears and your dreams. Evidence shows that a good, solid relationship will not only make you happier, it may even help you live longer.

HACK
#237

Spend Less Than You Earn

Many people see something they want and immediately buy it. If you do that over and over again, this philosophy can lead you into certain debt. Don't live beyond your means. Doing so has been proven to cause stress and anxiety; it also leads to conflicts among spouses or family members. Spending less than you earn in our materially driven society is not always easy, but the feelings of security and peace that come with not being in debt will certainly bring you more happiness than any purchase ever could.

Stargaze

Looking up at a sky full of stars is not only a meditative exercise that can help you feel more calm and centered, it also teaches you perspective. Contemplating the vastness and distance of space and the universe will help give you a new angle on your life and problems...and stargazing will help you discover the beauty of nature too. Stargazing can also be a kind of meditation; the calm peacefulness of gazing up at the stars can help quiet your mind and the stresses of your day. As an additional bonus the time spent outside, even as little as twenty minutes, will also be a big happiness booster.

HACK
#239

Don't Be Unhappy about Being Unhappy

There is pain in life. At some point in your glorious life, you will be unhappy, hurt, or depressed. These things are natural and are part of everyone's human experience. The most important thing during these times is to not beat yourself up about feeling the way you do. Feeling bad or embarrassed about feeling bad will not help you; in fact, those additional negative feelings may just drag you down even further. Instead, acknowledge your feelings—they are nothing to be ashamed of. Accepting the pain and difficulty of a situation is one of the ways to help yourself get out of it and back on the path to happiness.

HACK
#240

Break It Down

Our complex, busy lives only add to our stress and unhappiness. Break down the complexities of your day and find ways to simplify your life. Does your family really need more than one car? Do you need more than one credit card? Having more things in your life doesn't bring more freedom or happiness—in fact, in many cases, having more things limits these qualities. Your standard of life does not necessarily reflect your quality of life. If you simplify your life, the stresses of life will fade.

HACK
#241

Find a Silver Lining

People who are resilient are happier over the long term than people who aren't. We all get defeated sometimes, but people who are able to find some good in bad situations are more likely to thrive and find joy again. People who can take some actionable steps to focus not on their wounds but on how to make changes for the better (i.e., perhaps doing something they love or finding something good in their day) are able to grow from their experiences rather than being dragged down by them. Look for something to celebrate even in defeat, and you, too, will become a more resilient and happier person.

HACK
#242

Try to See Both Sides

Use conflict resolution techniques on a regular basis when you are dealing with conflicts and disagreements. For example, when trying to resolve a conflict, do so with a calm, thoughtful, and respectful demeanor. Show courtesy, kindness, empathy, and understanding. Listen to both sides and demonstrate your desire for a constructive solution. It may be necessary to restate the problem, paraphrasing it in your own words so that both sides are satisfied that you truly understand what's going on. Impress your desire to find a solution upon both parties. At all times, speak calmly and avoid being confrontational and aggressive. When the optimal solution is found, happiness and peace will again prevail.

Write Down the Steps to Your Goal

Think of five factors that are absolutely vital to the success of your goal. Write them on sticky paper or notecards and place them where you can see and think about them. For example, do you dream of starting your own business? Then you will have to know everything you can possibly know about your product and your ideal customers, have a business plan, find enough capital, and establish the proper price point for your product, for example. Knowing what is vital to the success of your goal will help you realistically reach your dreams.

HACK

#244

Record Your Relatives

Before a parent, grandparent, great aunt, or great uncle gets any older, ask him or her to join you for a recorded chat. Make it informal and begin with easy questions that can serve as points of departure into his or her story: When were you born? In what town, village, or city? Who were your parents? What kind of work did they do? Then ask open-ended questions: Can you tell me about your earliest memories? What was life like for you growing up in your town? Ask questions about certain periods in their life, such as their childhood, teen years, middle age, and golden years, for example. Once you've recorded those memories, even after your relative has passed away, you can relive those moments and feel joyful that you took the time to make the video.

Get a Mentor

Having a mentor can put you on the fast track in your job or propel your career into liftoff. Just asking someone to mentor you suggests to others that you are eager to move ahead and that you may even be an overachiever. If you have a career or job that requires special skills, why not seek out several mentors, one for each specialized area? Some career strategists believe that mentors are vital if you desire to rise quickly through the ranks. Plus, they can be wonderful allies to have as you pursue your dreams. A bonus is that both protégés and mentors seem to benefit from such relationships.

Join a Dating Site

If you're feeling lonely and that loneliness is making you unhappy, then do something about it. Visit a few online dating sites and research their audience demographics and their criteria for joining. Choose two or three sites that might allow you to find the type of potential partner you desire. Join one. While dating is still about meeting new people, dating sites make it easier than ever to meet those potential partners because you can state exactly what you are looking for. You just might meet some great people in the process!

HACK
#247

Try New Food or Drink

Next time you're traveling, sample some of the local cuisine—find a little restaurant that offers tapas or mezze or appetizers and try all of them. In the United Kingdom, go for some pub grub and a pint. In Belgium or Switzerland, tantalize your taste buds with some fine chocolate. Or for a really adventurous taste experience, try some haggis in Scotland or a plate of pickled pig's feet in northern Spain. Wherever you go, ask the locals about tasty regional specialties. If traveling abroad doesn't fit into your budget, grab a friend and go to a restaurant in your area that serves a cuisine you are unfamiliar with. Talk to your server about what he or she recommends and then go for it. Experiment and have fun!

Build a Nest Egg

Build a nest egg for yourself: open a traditional or Roth individual retirement account (IRA) and put the maximum amount that the IRS will allow into that account each year. But be wise about investing for your retirement—if you don't understand the differences between the two types of IRAs and the investment possibilities for growing your money (as well as the tax ramifications that go along with that), seek the counsel of a trusted financial advisor. It's all part of growing a bigger nest egg so that someday you can become a retiree with a lifestyle you love and can afford.

Take Five Deep Breaths

Calm the mind by breathing deeply five times from your belly, like you naturally did when you were a baby. Stop the mental thought chatter and just "be." Experience the present moment as it eternally renews itself in infinite diversity. To be mindful is to have an awareness of the moment without thinking or talking about it. By slowing the breath and thought, you will experience tranquility and happiness.

HACK #250

Use Your Delay for Good

When your train doesn't arrive on time or your flight is delayed, see the opportunities—get out your laptop or a notepad and make a list of positive things that could come about because of the delay. Think of that "stolen time" as a blessing that gives you extra time to use in myriad ways. You could:

- Make some phone calls
- Catch up on paperwork
- Study a map
- Brainstorm some new adventures
- Write some postcards, emails, or posts

HACK
#251

Quiet Your Mind

Focus on your thinking at the start of every day. Are you already mentally racing through your to-do list? Are your thoughts jumping from one subject to another thanks to thought associations? Did a troubling dream leave you anxious or angry or fearful upon awakening? If you answered yes to any of these questions, spend ten minutes doing a mental check-in before you even get out of bed. Take deep breaths and be aware of your entire body. Feel anchored and centered in it. Quiet your mind. Think positive thoughts. Dial out the emotions of bad dreams and the anxieties associated with the day ahead. Relax into peace. The world can wait for ten minutes.

Ask about Someone's Purpose in Life

If you've ever asked someone what their purpose in life is, you may have gotten a blank stare and silence. It's not like asking people to tell you what their job is. They are going through the motions of their lives and they know what they do every day—especially at their places of employment—but the word in your question that has thrown them off is "purpose." Purpose is the reason for doing something or why it exists. Working at a job is necessary to earn money, but it isn't your purpose. Living purposefully means much more than your job. Here's a hint: purpose likely will have something to do with love, compassion, peace, consciousness, truthfulness, meaning, awakening, or courage. Figure out your purpose, too, and then spark a dialogue on that topic with others. People are happiest when life has meaning and purpose for them.

Promote Yourself

When you feel passionate about a hobby, whether it is painting murals on the walls of children's rooms, sculpting bowls from driftwood, or making cigar box shrines, tell your friends and other hobby enthusiasts about your latest project. Word gets around. You may attract people who want to see your projects and perhaps even purchase your services or products. Post photos of your creations on social networking sites. You never know what wonderful opportunities may come your way when you put aside false modesty and instead promote yourself and your passion for your particular hobby.

Be an Organ Donor

You can save someone's life through donation of your vital organs after you've passed on by signing up with the organ registry in your state and by letting the Department of Motor Vehicles know your wishes the next time you renew your license. Registering to be an organ donor is easy and can make a huge difference for an individual fighting for his or her life as well as that person's family. Live happier knowing that at your life's end, the organs you no longer need can give someone else a fighting chance to live.

Read a Funny Book to a Kid

If you love to read, spend some time reading to children. You can read books to kids anywhere: at home, at a local library, at an infant and toddler day-care center, at a nursery school, in a doctor's or dentist's waiting room, in a hospital waiting room, or even at kids' organizations like the Cub Scouts or Brownies. Just be sure that your book is appropriate for the age group. A funny book will inspire laughter, and you'll likely laugh too—the happy laughter of children is infectious.

Get to Know Your Neighbors

When you meet a neighbor while, say, you're out walking your dog, say hello. Invite her to go grab some coffee. Get to know her. That means finding out what is important to her, what her hobbies are, what kind of work she does. Find out what mutual interests you share. From that beginning, you can build friendships with your neighbors.

HACK
#257

Follow the 60 Percent Rule

Perfection isn't possible. But many people pursue perfectionism with such vigor that it can actually be damaging. It's time to readjust that thinking. According to the 60 percent rule, if your friendships, work life, and relationships are 60 percent "perfect," then you are doing something right. Keep up the good work! Pushing for perfectionism will cause you unneeded stress and anxiety—instead, embrace the imperfect and feel happier.

HACK #258

Find Your Tribe

There is a certain kind of happiness that comes from finding people who understand you and your goals and who support and accept you. Go out there and find your tribe! Look around your community, check local *Meetup* groups, investigate *Facebook* groups, visit spiritual centers, join discussion groups…you can find communal possibilities for almost any area of interest. If you've had issues with addiction, 12-step groups made up of people who have been where you've been and who know the struggles you face have been proven to be pivotal to eventually overcoming addiction. The wonderful thing is that, based on your interests and needs, you can have more than one tribe. Find some like-minded people who truly "get" you, and you'll feel the happiness of acceptance.

HACK #259

Keep Your Sense of Humor

The best way to feel better and deal with pain is to have a sense of humor about life and yourself—when you are in the midst of a crisis, finding something funny can help. Not that you are expected to crack jokes in the middle of a crisis, but finding a bit of humor amidst the pain will bring you some relief. And if you can make others laugh a bit, too, all the better.

HACK #260

Feel Good about You

Feel good about what you've accomplished in life or the special talents you possess. Feeling good will help you find your true colors! Be proud of your uniqueness—don't try to bury it to fit in with a crowd. Suppressing what is natural and good about yourself will only lead to unhappiness. Be proud of the individual you are.

Ask for Help

Don't just reach out for help or support when things are in crisis—also reach out when you are working toward a goal and need help. Ask a friend or coworker to share their experience. This in turn will make the person you are asking feel valued, plus you will gain some of their knowledge and wisdom. Use that to help make your dream come true.

Realize That Happiness Comes from Within

Often people pin their hopes on external conditions that are out of their control, or they underestimate their power to control their own happiness. Never forget the power of the mind to generate happiness! The mind can make you feel miserable even if you're living in paradise, or the mind can make you feel happy even in the midst of adversity. Make your mind your best friend rather than your enemy, and happiness will follow.

Smell Something That Makes You Happy

Smell isn't just a fragrance; it's a memory—think about chocolate-chip cookies baking in your grandma's oven or a bouquet of flowers that a special date gave you. Because olfactory responses are directly linked to the emotional centers of the brain, they cause a flood of warm and fuzzy feelings that are sure to boost your mood. Find your favorite fragrance and smell it to increase your happiness.

Challenge Yourself

Challenges are opportunities for growth and are one of the keys to happiness. Having something to strive for will keep you out of the negativity rut, so do something you've always wanted try (even if you're afraid to do it). Find something that gives you a sense of purpose and then strive for it.

Get Lost in a Book

Find a beloved book that makes you laugh or cry or sigh every time you read it, curl up in a quiet, sunny place with it, and get lost in the story. Let yourself be lifted out of your own life and into the world of the book. Share the characters' triumphs and feel their torments. Escape your own problems for a little while. True, you can't run away from issues in real life, but sometimes the respite of a good story can lighten your mood and give you a much-needed break to clear your mind. This works with your favorite movie too!

Do Something Unexpected

Our brains take pleasure in new and novel ideas. To encourage you to seek out the new and unexpected, your brain will release feel-good hormones when you try something new. Routines bring stagnation—it's time to break out of your rut and find some joy! Try something you normally wouldn't and then feel the rush of happiness. Maybe you've always wanted to skydive or kayak or drive off to that inn by the beach…whatever it is, try it!

Get Up for the Sunrise

The most magical times of the day often go by unnoticed. There is something so beautiful and peaceful about the sunrise! Try waking up early one morning to go out and witness it. Hear the quiet chirp of the early birds, feel the breeze on your face, watch as the sunlight first appears over the horizon and begins the day with its light. A sunrise is akin to a religious experience—don't miss it. Watch a sunrise just once, and you'll notice how positive you feel for the whole rest of the day.

HACK #268

Avoid Drama Queens

Some people love to cause trouble—they love to interfere in situations that are not really their concern and stir the pot of emotions. Whether they do so out of a desire to create chaos and push other people's buttons or to boost their own egos by making themselves feel superior, if you want to hold on to your happiness, you should avoid these types of people at all costs. Toxic people have a need to suck others into their negative spiral. Avoid the drama and distance yourself from them! If you can't turn a person's focus away from negativity, then simply excuse yourself and leave the conversation. Your happiness is worth the little bit of awkward interaction you might need to initiate to remove yourself from the situation.

HACK #269

Spend a Day Alone

"Me time" is a concept that is slowly slipping away in our hectic world, but it's critical for your mental health. For just one day, try to spend that day with only yourself—no family, no friends, no coworkers. While these people may have your best intentions in mind, they are often a distraction from getting to know your real self. Spend a day relaxing, doing the things you love, eating foods that make you happy, and focusing on you and your purpose. Avoid checking your phone at all. Really unplug yourself from the world. It won't be as awful as you may think! In fact, the peace that comes from occasional solitude will make you feel refreshed and calm.

Do Something You Loved As a Kid

Nostalgia and reminiscing stimulate those feel-good emotions because they make your brain remember how happy you were when you first did the things you're remembering. Think back to something you really loved doing as a kid. Roller skating? Playing at the beach? Eating ice cream at the ice cream parlor? Visiting a relative's house? Whatever it is, find a way to do it again. Sure, the experience will be slightly different now that you are a bit older and time has passed, but the joy you'll get by reliving your favorite memories will be the same. When kids do fun things, they aren't embarrassed or shy or intimidated—they simply experience the richness of life. Go be a kid again! You'll reignite the joy that came from having those experiences.

Tackle Change

We all have a resistance to change when things come up that may alter our comfortable way of living. One way to battle this resistance is to make small changes—even tiny changes help. Say there's something you have been resisting doing. Try doing it for just five minutes. Anyone can do something for five minutes, right? Research new careers for just five minutes. Walk or paint or play an instrument for just five minutes. The goal of these short bursts of time is to find something related to doing that activity that brings you joy. Doing something you hate is possible for a while, but you'll never stick with it—you need to find some joy in an activity in order to keep on doing it. That's why you need to find something—anything—that makes you happy about that activity. Once you have, then you'll be able to change.

HACK
#272

React with Sincere Enthusiasm

This hack harkens back to the fact that when you bring happiness to others, you will feel happy yourself. Just remember: it's important to be sincere and give active and constructive responses. We live in a world where people show their responses in emojis and symbols, which in reality are empty and meaningless. If someone shares good news with you, send a sincere response that shows genuine interest in and happiness for the other person. By doing so, you will create stronger social bonds and give people a more positive view of you.

HACK
#273

Put Yourself First

When it comes to your life, the only person you really have control over is yourself. Other people in your life influence you and bring you happiness and joy and security, but you have no control over their choices or destinies. Of course, you love these people, and you'll accomplish many things and make many sacrifices to help them when they are in need. But when you are in crisis, you must put yourself before anyone else. Focus on what you need to get through your situation. You may not be able to help others right now, and that's okay—you will be there for them another time. If you spend your time focusing on others and making sure they are okay, you will be mistreating the most important person in your life: yourself.

HACK
#274

Call Your Mom

Oftentimes life takes over our focus, and we forget the people who helped shape us into the independent and self-assured adults we are today. No matter how old you are or where you live, your mom will always worry about how you're doing. Call her! Actually call her—don't message her or send her a text. Call her and let her hear your voice. Your mom will feel loved and cherished, and you'll feel great too.

Nap

Seniors and two-year-olds have the right idea: on some days, a nap is one of the greatest pleasures you can find. Being able to break away from the hectic pace of life in the middle of the day and lying down to rest will leave you feeling rejuvenated and ready to tackle the rest of your day. Besides, many of us are not getting enough sleep during the standard nighttime hours—we all could use a bit more rest! Even a quick power nap will do wonders for your mood and your day.

Don't Compare

If you're going to base your feeling of self-worth on feeling superior to others, you'll be frustrated for most of your life. It's tempting to compare your accomplishments to those of others—we all do it from time to time as a way to motivate ourselves—but this kind of comparison is dangerous. Someone will always have more money or possessions than you do or be better at doing something than you are. Comparing creates a cycle of futility. The less you compare your life and accomplishments to those of others, the happier you'll be.

HACK
#277

Trust Strangers

Believing that people are out to cheat you causes unneeded stress and anxiety. If you are constantly worried that a cashier will shortchange you or that a coworker will try to steal the spotlight or that an acquaintance is talking about you behind your back, you won't be happy. The more you perceive that you can trust others, the happier you'll be. Of course, you shouldn't blindly trust people you don't know, but go in with a positive attitude and give others the benefit of the doubt.

HACK
#278

It's Not You
(No, Really)

We all face rejection at some point in life. Whether it happens in our professional or personal lives, it is easy to see the rejection as a personal affront. But sometimes rejections aren't personal, and sometimes they don't really have much to do with you as an individual; sometimes the timing just isn't right. Sure, it can be frustrating to see your boss reject the idea you spent months growing and grooming, but it happens. And when it does, try to see the rejection as a learning opportunity rather than as a rejection of you as a person. You will find more success and happiness if you can keep your ego out of the process and view the situation for what it is.

HACK
#279

Pay Attention

We are always striving for more and adding more things into our lives, and that can lead to us ignoring the good things we have right now. When something good comes your way, you should pay attention to it. You should experience it and savor it. Too often, we ignore the good in our lives in our relentless pursuit of the better. We tell ourselves we won't be happy until X or Y happens, and in the meantime, we miss the good we have already achieved. Pay attention to the good you have already have and feel the happiness it brings.

HACK
#280

Take Care of Your Body

Physical problems can affect your emotional state. If you are experiencing a small pain, ache, or discomfort in your body, address it now: get a massage, see a physical therapist, go to a doctor. Small physical pains can grow over time and start to affect your life in negative ways. Remove these pains from your life to create a happier emotional state.

HACK

#281

Stop Being Distracted

Distractions are nice every now and again—they take our minds off our troubles and allow us to rest and recuperate without having to think too much. However, distractions start to be a problem when they are distracting you so much that you are losing hours of your day to diversions instead of tending to the things that matter in your life. That video game, those Internet articles, those *Facebook* posts…they're fun, but they will not bring you real happiness. Distract yourself only in moderation and don't risk sacrificing the meaningful parts of your life.

HACK #282

Let Go of Negative Body Images

There is no one "correct" body type. Sure, you should strive to be as healthy as you can, but if you feel comfortable in your own skin and you're happy with your life, don't let other people's opinions of body types get in your head. Don't let other people tell you you're not beautiful or that you could be more beautiful if you only did this or that. Your opinion of your body is the only one that matters. If you are not happy in your own skin, then take steps to improve yourself, but only if you truly desire to make those changes.

HACK #283

Stop Thinking Good Things Will Just Fall Into Your Lap

You cannot be idle in your own life and just wait and hope that good things will come your way by coincidence—no one who has experienced good fortune has achieved it coincidentally. You must take an active role in the world and your life if you want good things to happen. Be grateful for what you have and appreciate all you have accomplished, but never stop striving to make the most out of your life.

HACK #284

Be Optimistic about the Future

None of us know what the future holds, but if you can remain optimistic about the future and your ability to accomplish your goals, then you will be happier. Surround yourself with people who nurture and support your optimism. Having a naysayer in your life who constantly tries to redirect you away from your goals or make you feel embarrassed about them will only tarnish your outlook. Nurture positive relationships with people who help lift you up.

Seek Out a Life Coach

If you are experiencing obstacles to happiness and you can't figure out how to overcome those obstacles, a life coach might be able to help you. Life coaches can help you evaluate your life and determine what you're not happy about. Maybe you are sabotaging your own happiness without even realizing it! Talking with a life coach can help you discover what you can do better (or stop doing) so that you can live a happier life.

Forgive Your Stumbles

We all screw up. The secret to being able to handle life's stumbles is to forgive yourself. You'll encounter setbacks, and when you do, you should not give up or become despondent—instead, tackle the setbacks. If you are doing the right thing most of the time, then you are doing pretty well. No one can make it through life without a few stumbles along the way, so forgive yourself for having made those errors and move on.

HACK
#287

Think about the Worst

This may seem like a contrary statement considering all the advice in this book about focusing on the good in life, but when you are faced with a frightening or anxiety-riddled situation and you cannot force yourself to find the good in it, sometimes the best plan is to focus on the worst outcome. Figure out the very worst thing that could happen as a result of the situation and think about how badly things could go (in detail). In most cases, you're going to discover that your anxiety about the situation is exaggerated.

HACK
#288

Try After-Dinner Gratitude

Each night after dinner, write down five good things that happened to you during the day. Most people are tired after a long day at work and can tend to drift toward the negative, but by doing this exercise, you can redirect your mood toward the things that are going well and thus increase your positivity. Pause for a few minutes to write down the things that went just the way you'd planned or perhaps some small surprises during the day that put a smile on your face. Writing down these gratitudes may sound trivial, but journaling this way has been proven to reduce stress and redirect people out of negative cycles.

Don't Censor Yourself

All too often, we hide ourselves behind a mask of who we think we are supposed to be. Stop censoring your life and say what you really think! Don't worry about what other people may think of you. Of course, don't hurl hate at other people—rather, just don't be afraid to say what you feel about yourself and your desires. Don't concern yourself about whether or not others are going to like your opinions or thoughts. They can have their own opinions on the matter. Feel free to express yourself the way you like, without concern for other people's desires.

Be Curious

There is so much to experience and learn about in life! You can't help but be in awe of the world and its wonders. Be curious and explore. Never stop questioning why things are a certain way. Learn something new, read something new, try something new. Never lose your curiosity about life.

Get Rid of Things That Drag You Down

Moderation may work in some cases, but if something is not bringing you joy, why are you keeping it around? Get rid of anything that robs you of happiness. And don't get rid of it gradually—get rid of it cold turkey. Make a list of things that zap your energy, slow you down, or leave you feeling guilty or remorseful, and then simply cut them out of your life. That may not be easy to do, but your increased joy and feelings of well-being will be worth it.

Do the Hard Stuff First

If you finish your most difficult task first, then the rest of your day will be easier and more productive. As humans, we tend to procrastinate and put off the things we don't want to do, but if you can get the things you dread out of the way first, you won't be anxious. That lack of anxiety will greatly improve your day.

Learn to Fight Smarter

When you are engaged in a heated argument and people are screaming at each other, is there really ever a winner? Or are there just two sides who are angry and bitter and deaf to the other side's opinions? Fight smarter, not harder. Engage the other person in rational and nonaggressive ways so that you can both communicate your opinions clearly. Listen to what your opponent is saying and then try to summarize and restate their thoughts aloud so that they know you have heard them. We all have to deal with conflict, but you don't have to explode to get your point across.

Decide Not to Be Frustrated

Want to feel happier and less frustrated with the minutiae of daily life? Then decide not to get frustrated by all the little things that don't go as planned. Raise your frustration tolerance so that you don't let frustration take over and ruin your day. Don't get mad when little irritations pop up—instead, try and find the humor in them. Just go with it and roll with the punches. You'll be happier!

Don't Judge

No matter what you see on the surface, you can never know what another person is really going through. We often tend to judge and criticize others without even knowing it. Yet when you do that, you are coming from a place of jealousy or fear, and that is not demonstrating your best self. You have no idea about the journey other people have gone through or what they've experienced to make them who they are today. You have no right to criticize what you don't understand. Besides, judging others will limit your happiness as well. You wouldn't want to feel judged, right? So don't judge others.

HACK

#296

Smile at Yourself

It may sound silly, but smiling causes an emotional response in your body that can actually make you feel happier. Smiling at other people can make them and you feel happier, but smiling at yourself in the mirror can have the added effect of boosting your self-esteem and self-love. Imagine smiling at yourself in the mirror every morning—think about what that would do for your confidence and mood throughout the day!

HACK

#297

Be Grateful for Your Problems

You have problems now, and you will probably always have some kind of problems in your life—as old ones disappear, new ones emerge. But it's how you view your problems that determines whether or not they will overtake you. Focus on your problems, and they will seem huge; focus on the good things in your life, and your problems will seem smaller. You should also try (this may be harder at some times than others) to appreciate your problems. Sure, they may seem frustrating today, but tomorrow they could turn into an opportunity you hadn't thought of.

HACK
#298

Give Yourself More Time

One of the biggest sources of frustration in our busy lives is being late and all the annoying distractions that can lead to that. Stuck in traffic? Missed a bus? Burned your breakfast? So much frustration and anxiety can be avoided if you allow yourself extra time to get places and to get stuff done. Wake up earlier in the morning to allow for traffic, for example—then you won't be late for work and have your boss glaring at you all day. Pace yourself. You'll have a more relaxed and happier day!

HACK #299

Keep Your Mouth Shut

Can you feel that snarky comment hovering on your lips, about to burst forth at your significant other's expense? Hold it in. Feel angry at your boss and know that your anger is about to become a tirade? Keep your mouth shut. The old saying is true: once you've said something, you can't take it back. If you feel you are about to say something you'll regret later, just don't say it. This will prevent a huge amount of potential trouble! Keeping your mouth shut will save your relationships too.

HACK #300

Be Kind to Unkind People

Don't be a martyr or a pushover by any means, but when you see the office jerk who always gives everyone problems, try being kind. Ask him about his day or his family or joke about the latest office escapade. Unkind people often need kindness the most. Of course, some people are just negative and no amount of your kindness will help them, but you will feel better about yourself knowing you tried. And maybe your little bit of kindness will change the other person's day, after all.

HACK
#301

Take the Higher Road

If you want to be happier, you must realize that some conflicts are unnecessary and a waste of your time. Some people are toxic and are so addicted to drama and anger that you will never win an argument with them or even reach a common understanding. There are far too many fun and wonderful things to spend your time on—you don't need to fight every battle. Try to reach an understanding with someone you are arguing with, but if it's going nowhere, make your own day better: remove yourself from the situation and prevent yourself from being sucked into their drama.